THE
INDESCRIBABLE
CHRIST

VOLUMES IN THIS SERIES

THE INDESCRIBABLE CHRIST

*The Names and Titles of
Jesus Christ
A.B.C.D.E.F.G.*

by Charles J. Rolls

LOIZEAUX BROTHERS

Neptune, New Jersey

REVISED EDITION, JANUARY 1984
FOURTH PRINTING, OCTOBER 1988

Library of Congress Cataloging in Publication Data

Rolls, Charles J. (Charles Jubilee), 1887-
  The indescribable Christ: The names and titles of
Jesus Christ: A—G. Revised edition.

  Previously published: Grand Rapids: Zondervan Pub.
House, 1953.

  1. Jesus Christ—Names.   I. Title.   II. Series:
Rolls, Charles J. (Charles Jubilee), 1887—   Names
and titles of Jesus Christ.
BT590.N2R6   1983   232   83-19890
ISBN 0-87213-731-7

PRINTED IN THE UNITED STATES OF AMERICA

*This book is dedicated to
my late wife
Frances Rolls
who was most helpful
during the writing of it
in 1952*

CONTENTS

A

B

C

D

E

F

G

FOREWORD

Early in the present century, when he discovered the atom, the New Zealand scientist, Viscount Rutherford, said in the course of one of his lectures on the subject, "The terms we utilize when describing small things, such as 'little,' 'tiny,' and 'mite,' are far too big in their suggestiveness for expressing the nature of the atom." It is even more true that the words "colossal," "massive," and "gigantic" are far too small in their descriptiveness to convey an adequate estimate of the fullness of the measure of the stature of Christ. The stateliness of His personality and the magnitude of His spiritual dignity cast their radiance athwart the entire universe. If it were within the range of possibility to remove all trace of the record of the manifestation of Christ from the annals of history, the whole world would be bereft, and mankind would lose the one sole expression of effulgent light, essential love and eternal life.

Christ is the only One of all those who ever appeared on this earth who wielded the powers of Providence, swayed the scepter of omnipotence and exercised the full faculties of omniscience. Without Him, the hope we cherish of a permanent peace would perish and the radiance of a ratified redemption from ruin would vanish. Apart from His victory over the grave, the ravages of the devil and the rampage of death would continue to flourish through the corridors of time without any prospect of cessation. We should remember also, that it was Christ the Creator who determined the bounds of national habitation, diverted the stream of civilization from its channel and deflected the trend of human aspiration from the terrestrial to the celestial. At present He is at home amid the high noon of heaven's summertide, preparing a place of habitation for the multitudes of His redeemed people.

11

The skill of the experts cannot account for His perfect spiritual manhood, nor can the wisdom of the philosophers expound the preciousness of His sacrificial shepherdhood. Even the foremost sages of science seem to stall when they attempt to elucidate the rays of supernatural light which emanate from the pellucid purity of His glorious priesthood. Paul, the most profound of the theologians, comprehended the inner secret of this ineffable mystery when he declared, "God was in Christ, reconciling the world unto Himself" (II Cor. 5:19); and again in a personal application of the same He said, "The Son of God, who loved me, and gave Himself for me" (Gal. 2:20). The Apostle Peter recognized the priceless truth of these realities when he wrote, "For Christ also hath once suffered for sins, the just for the unjust, that He might bring us to God" (I Pet. 3:18). The treasures of His amazing love perfume the ineffable glory, and the trophies of His indestructible peace crown the unwithering beauty of the kingdom of God. From among the many constellations of the starry sublimities of Christ, we submit this cluster of His celebrated capacities — a selection of but eighty-four of His conspicuous titles, names and offices.

CHARLES J. ROLLS

A

These names present Christ in the majesty of His greatness and in stately relationships of ability and achievement, wherein He stands absolutely alone, as Author and Administrator.

The AUTHOR OF SALVATION (Heb. 5:9)
> Christ holds exclusive requisites for essential authorship.

The ANCIENT OF DAYS (Dan. 7:9)
> The ageless, timeless, changeless One.

The ALMIGHTY WHICH IS (Rev. 1:8)
> Christ is faultless and flawless in His exercise of might.

The ARM OF THE LORD (Isa. 53:1)
> Adequately able to administer authority.

The ANGEL OF THE COVENANT (Mal. 3:1)
> He came to confirm the promise and fulfill the purpose.

The ARK OF THE LORD (Josh. 3:3)
> The gracious Guide and glorious Guardian.

The ADVOCATE WITH THE FATHER (I John 2:1)
> Christ assures access and acceptance.

The ANCHOR OF HOPE (Heb. 6:19)
> He is strength for our effort and the stay of expectancy.

The APOSTLE AND HIGH PRIEST (Heb. 3:1)
> Fully obedient in observing obligations.

The ALTOGETHER LOVELY (Song of Sol. 5:16)
> The highest and holiest in loveliness.

The AMEN (Rev. 3:14)
> Faithful and final in fulfilling God's Word.

The ALL, AND IN ALL (Col. 3:11)
> Christ more than superabounds in all-sufficiency.

13

CHRIST IS ALL

Christ is

not a fragment of the Divine but the Fullness of Deity
not a temporary shadow but the True Substance
not a provisional makeshift but a Perfect Manifestation
not a social organizer but the Saviour of Mankind
not a world reformer but a Wondrous Redeemer
not a Jewish shepherd but Jehovah Shaloam
not a figment of reason but the Fountain of Revelation

AND IN ALL

Oh Christ! there is no greater fame than Thine,
  Which history's pages have engraved in gold;
No record of great deeds could e'er outshine
  The princely labors of Thy love untold.

Oh Christ! there is no sweeter theme than Thine,
  That heralds to a restless world God's peace;
No truth nor tidings ever did enshrine
  So grand a message of such full release.

Oh Christ! there is no dearer name than Thine,
  Which time hath blazoned on its mighty scroll;
No wreath or garland ever did entwine
  So fair a temple of so vast a soul.

Oh Christ! there is no stronger love than Thine,
  More strong than death and mightier than the grave;
That triumphed over sin with grace divine
  And brought to man God's matchless power to save.

Oh Christ! there is no brighter home than Thine,
  Which bids us welcome to its mansions fair;
Amid the treasures that are superfine
  We share the glories with Thyself, the Heir.

Oh Christ! there is no wiser plan than Thine,
  Founding a kingdom none can undermine
Thy very self, the chief foundation stone;
  With fadeless glory that is all Thine own.

Oh Christ! there is no higher throne than Thine,
Replete in holiness of truth subline;
Where beauty, purity, and love combine
In perfect righteousness, with joy divine.

I am Alpha and Omega (Rev. 22:13)

The greatness and majesty of Christ are utterly inconceivable. Though in the saintliest spiritual state, the most masterly minds have felt how impossible it is to conceive the grandeur of God and the glory of the Father as revealed in the character of Christ Jesus our Lord. Our research in astronomy and anatomy is ever furnishing exceptional marvels in the material and physical realms by opening to the mind of man the illimitable fields in the handiwork of God that exist for human investigation. In such things we view but a tiny patch in the vast mosaic of the Maker's works. This Potter, however, is infinitely greater than the vessels He has fashioned and the designs He has framed. Immensity and eternity cannot encompass Him; He is the product of neither, for how can there be pedigree or ancestry in the case of the Infinite One? The Scripture affirms "The heaven of heavens cannot contain Thee" (I Kings 8:27). Yet withal we hear the wonderful declaration from above, "Thus saith the high and lofty One that inhabiteth eternity, whose name is Holy; I dwell in the high and holy place, with him also that is of a contrite and humble spirit, to revive the spirit of the humble, and to revive the heart of the contrite ones" (Isa. 57:15).

Our purpose is to occupy our minds in meditation on the range and renown of Christ's glory as set forth in this profound claim, "I am Alpha and Omega," encompassing as it does the whole alphabet, which is the key of all literature in any given language. The implication in the use Christ makes of it is, "I am the whole revelation of God." No aspect of Christ's life or ministry dims the luster of any single feature of the attributes of God, whom He resembles and represents completely. In Christ all the divine attributes are perfectly balanced, this being seen equally in His matchless kindness, His stainless pureness, His peerless loveliness, His blameless justness, His flawless righteousness, His faultless meekness, His fadeless faithfulness, His staunchless goodness, His priceless preciousness, His boundless blessedness, His taintless truthfulness, His spotless holiness, and the thirty remaining characteristics which we know are included in the character of Godhead. "God was in Christ, reconciling the world unto Himself" (II Cor. 5:19). Everyone of the attributes expressed in the manifestation and ministry of Christ contributes to the glory of God. Not one of the perfections of God in Christ neutralizes or nullifies any other attribute. True it is that some stress His love as though it had a preponderance in His character and stood out as most conspicuous of all; but far more space is given in Scripture to the description and declaration of His righteousness than of His love. Nor are these two features at variance; they blend beautifully and work harmoniously together.

I asked the Lord to show me something of the wonderful meaning incorporated in that astounding claim, "I am Alpha and Omega." I am convinced that no mind is big enough to comprehend the magnitude of the measureless range of dignity and glory embodied in such a stupendous claim. However, we may go through each letter of the Alphabet and make a selection of two or three hundred of Christ's titles, offices, vocations and names that appear on the surface. Let us begin by suggesting some of His designations which commence with the letter "A."

THE AUTHOR OF SALVATION

> And being made perfect, He became the author of eternal salvation unto all them that obey Him (Heb. 5:9; also 12:2).

In His authorship Christ precedes all others; in origination He stands supreme and pre-eminent, without peer or competitor. No other authorship could possibly be appended to this supremely important subject of salvation. The Prophet Isaiah records in his message, "I, even I, am the LORD; and beside Me there is no saviour" (Isa. 43:11). Hosea also repeats the same assurance, "For there is no saviour beside Me" (Hos. 13:4). We may name a multitude of authors in connection with literature and lexicons, history and homilies, dictionaries and declarations, encyclopedias and encyclicals, but there is only one Author of Salvation. In this greatest of all author-ships Christ stands absolutely and eternally alone, "Neither is there salvation in any other: for there is none other name under heaven given among men, whereby we must be saved" (Acts 4:12). Likewise He is the sole Author of the faith which appropriates the salvation, "For by grace are ye saved through faith; and that not of yourselves: it is the gift of God" (Eph. 2:8).

In order to qualify for the authorship of eternal salvation it is essential that the one who plans the project should know all about everything, be able to do anything and be available everywhere to undertake for anyone and everyone always and altogether. This means nothing short of possessing the at-tributes of omniscience, omnipotence and omnipresence. Christ, who exercises these infinite powers, is therefore eminently fitted, expressly suited and eternally qualified to be the Saviour.

Our Lord's pre-eminent suitability and perfect capacity as Author are conclusively revealed in the Scriptures of truth. He already holds exclusive distinction in endless perfectness, as Author of eternal ages and of abiding life. He is fitted in the fullest sense to be our Substitute. He is definitely suited by virtue of His superior sufficiency to satisfy the heart and mind, and He is most qualified by reason of His sovereign strength to perfect forever them that are sanctified. The whole of His saving work is warranted in the light of His own worthiness. His holiness and honor stand highest in heaven. The salvation Christ accomplished does not depend on human behavior but on the beloved Saviour Himself, for "He became the author of eternal salvation unto all them that obey Him" (Heb. 5:9). Nor does this speak of a transient deliverance from temporal troubles and trivialities, but of deliverance from the domain of the Devil and from the dominion of sin and death forever. The pledge was formerly made, "Israel shall be saved in the LORD, with an everlasting salvation" (Isa. 45:17). Therefore, we can safely say that His will determined the purpose, His wisdom planned it, His work wrought it and His own Word declared it finished.

The perfect suitability of His precious blood for propitiation supplies a permanent basis for the peace of salvation; the invaluable ministry of His intercession, which rests upon His indestructibility, insures permanence for salvation even to the uttermost (Heb. 7:25); while the credentials of His consecration pave the way for our acceptance in a ceaseless communion, holy and without blame before Him in love (Eph. 1:4; Heb. 7:25). Our blessed Saviour is admittedly, adequately and adorably the Author of Salvation.

THE ANCIENT OF DAYS

> I beheld till the thrones were cast down, and the Ancient of Days did sit, whose garment was white as snow, and the hair of His head like the pure wool (Dan. 7:9).

Christ is not described here as the Ancient of Years, which would imply age, but Ancient of Days, which indicates His ageless, timeless, changeless character. No furrows disfigure His graceful features, no defects mar His clear discernment, nor is there any weakness in His wondrous will. His body of glory and beauty of countenance are unwrinkled by years, while His vigorous vitality and virtuous energy are unwearied by ceaseless activity. Ages are absolutely unable to age this ageless One who abides unchanged, "The same yesterday, and today, and forever" (Heb. 13:8). The march of seasons cannot mar His fairness nor foul weather destroy His freshness, for He has the dew of His youth (Ps. 110:3). The centuries cannot change His comeliness nor cramp His competence, for He is immune from infirmity and inured to infinity.

Pre-eminence belongs to the Ancient of Days by virtue of His priority and precedence, combined with the permanence of immortal perfection. Christ is the embodiment of the glories of Godhead, embracing the treasures of truth, the loveliness of light and the splendors of sublimity that never age, but form part of His lasting heritage. A myriad of marvels manifest themselves out of His exhaustless storehouse; yet no diminution of His resource is occasioned. If we contemplate the prescient eye of His providential care, the patient ear of His paternal interest, the prevalent grace of His prevailing goodness, the profound delights of His precious promises, the permanent security of His protecting hand and the plentiful supply of His perfect strength, we discover that all of these characteristics are but the abiding attributes of the Ancient of Days. None of these realities grows stale but is just as fresh and full and free as ever. The emerald throne of His majesty symbolizes the evergreen nature of His amaranthine beauty.

He is as young as the morning, although it be of ancient origin. He is as youthful as daybreak, a feature which thrilled our earliest ancestors. He who shielded Abraham, sustained Elijah and stayed the plague in Israel is the One who is and was and is to come, the Ancient of Days, even the Almighty. His energy knows nothing of exhaustion and His freshness never faces fatigue. The brilliance of His brightness never blurs, the sunlike sheen of His sympathetic face never shadows and the sufficiency of His saving strength never stalls, His "hand is not shortened, that it cannot save" (Isa. 59:1).

We may adopt garnished oratory to attract attention and elaborate with seraphic eloquence to awaken admiration, but how paltry is our best phraseology compared with one glimpse of the Ancient of Days.

> Show me Thy face, one transient gleam
>   Of loveliness divine,
> And I shall never think or dream
>   Of other love save Thine.
> All lesser lights shall lessen quite,
>   All lower glories wane,
> The beautiful of earth shall scarce
>   Seem beautiful again.

THE ALMIGHTY

The Lord, which is, and which was, and which is to
come, the Almighty (Rev. 1:8).

The strength of Christ's might and the majesty of His
stability transcend all others and all else in ability and
authority, for His is omnipotent. At this point we are to
consider Christ as the competent, independent, self-sufficient
One in His almightiness. The grand title which appears forty-
eight times in the Old Testament is here applied to our
Redeemer. The magnificence of the name in its depth of
meaning and degree of might, defies the capacity of our
reasoning powers. Superficially we comprehend its import,
but actually we do not. The Almighty is supremely real,
dispassionately true and faultlessly just; yet withal infinitely
tender and graciously kind, as revealed in the Book of Job,
where the title occurs thirty-one times.

His almightiness is expressed alike in the material, physical,
spiritual and judicial realms. This feature may also be applied
to His sublimity of thought, stability of mind, sovereignty of
will, sufficiency of wisdom, security of power, suitability of
grace and serenity of peace, in all of which He is the Almighty.
When we pause to ponder His enormous energy, His
prodigious power, His stupendous strength and marvelous
might, these ponderous quantities of ableness, with their
tremendous potential, cause us to tremble at the thought of
meeting such forces in exercise; but when we turn and learn of
the blended qualities of goodness demonstrated in the
character of divine activity, we behold the gracious care,
generous pity, gorgeous gifts and glorious love which are
lavished so freely, and our fears depart for we view His heart.
This is exactly what Job longed for when, discouraged and
downcast, he concluded God had decided to despise the work
of His hands (Job 10:3), hands which he knew to be characterized by wisdom and strength (Job 12:9-13). Job was
definitely corrected in his mistaken ideas by Elihu who
declared, "Behold, God is mighty, and despiseth not any: He
is mighty in strength and wisdom" (Job 36:5).

All things emanate from His creative wisdom and are maintained by His sustaining strength. Round about us many demonstrations illustrate the magnanimity of God as expressed by Elihu. For instance, the sun is too majestic to despise a worm, the ocean is too gigantic to disdain a sprat, the rain is too prolific to disregard a leaf, and "behold, God is mighty, and despiseth not any." He is "mighty in battle" (Ps. 24:8). "I am poor and needy; yet the Lord thinketh upon me" (Ps. 40:17).

THE ARM OF THE LORD

> Who hath believed our report? and to whom is the arm
> of the LORD revealed? (Isa. 53:1)

This striking figure is used as a great symbol of the delivering power and defending strength of the Lord Himself. The pronoun "He" immediately follows in the text. Thus the title attaches to Messiah. Thirty-six of the references to arm in the Old Testament are in relation to the Lord and His activities. Three of these from this same prophet will serve as an example. "On Mine arm shall they trust." "Put on strength, O arm of the Lord" (Isa. 51:5,9). "Mine own arm brought salvation" (Isa. 63:5). The One here represented is the Regent of providences, the Ruler of principalities and the Ratifier of the promises of God, all of which promises He came to confirm (Rom. 15:8). He is available for the tempted, the troubled, the tried and the tired. He is ready at hand to supply strength for the weak, help for the weary and cheer for the discouraged. In exercising His great power "He had done no violence" (Isa. 53:9). But He did use His might in ministry to the needy. He healed the sick, cleansed the lepers, forgave the sinners, discharged the debtors, delivered the captives, blessed the young, served the unfortunate, regarded the aged, defended the feeble, rewarded the diligent and beautified the meek.

> Under the shadow of Thy throne
> Thy saints have dwelt secure;
> Sufficient is Thine arm alone,
> And our defense is sure.
>
> ISAAC WATTS

In the Psalm of the Shepherd of Israel it is written, "Let Thy right hand be upon the man of Thy right hand, upon the son of man whom Thou madest strong for Thyself" (Ps. 80:17). We may add to this from the Covenant Psalm, "Thou hast a mighty arm; strong is Thy hand, and high is Thy right hand " (Ps. 89:13). The symbol of the arm of the Lord is one of the grandest Biblical figures of Christ's capability for command and conquest. He can bruise the head of the destroyer and break the bondage of darkness, as when He brought Israel out of Egypt (Exod. 6:6; Deut. 5:15). Christ sways the scepter of His imperial strength in every sphere of national and civil society. He is the Master of the mighty, the Captain of conquerors, the Head of heroes, the Leader of legislators, the Overseer of overcomers, the Governor of governors, the Prince of princes, the King of kings and the Lord of lords. As Administrator of celestial and terrestrial authority He is firm and fearless; none can resist His final judgment. The ages cannot atrophy the Arm of the Lord, "Behold, the Lord GOD will come with strong hand, and His arm shall rule for Him; behold, His reward is with Him, and His work before Him" (Isa. 40:10).

THE ANGEL OF THE COVENANT

> Behold, I will send My messenger, and he shall prepare the way before Me: and the Lord, whom ye seek, shall suddenly come to His temple, even the messenger (or angel) of the covenant, whom ye delight in: behold, He shall come (Mal. 3:1).

This precious designation is prominent throughout the history of Israel. Sometimes He is referred to as "the angel of God," to guide and guard (Exod. 14:19); on other occasions He appears as "the angel of His presence," to sympathize and save (Isa. 63:9), and frequently, "the angel of the LORD," to sustain and strengthen as in I Kings 19:7. In reflecting on some of these theophanies, as we may term them, we alight upon the distress of a mother and child facing the specter of a desperate death from thirst. Suddenly the Angel of God called and the tragedy was averted (Gen. 21:17).

> Say not my soul from whence shall God relieve thy care,
> Remember that omnipotence hath servants everywhere.

In His mission of mercy this Messenger often disguises His direct guidance in order to display His guardianship; "And the angel of God, which went before the camp of Israel, removed and went behind them" (Exod. 14:19). When Balak the son of Zippor and Balaam the hireling connived together to flash curses from the highest crags down on the camp of Israel, the Angel of the Lord was there to challenge their authority (Num. 22:34-35; 23:12). This very Messenger suits Himself to every season and occasion, and wherever His visits are recorded a reason for His appearing is given.

In the Book of Judges, where He plays a very prominent part, He is seen censuring sin at Bochim (Judg. 2:1-5), cursing cowards at Meroz (Judg. 5:23), or choosing special workmen for definite service (Judg. 6:11,12,20-22). Gideon the vigorous and venturesome, when vexed by marauding Midianites, heard the voice of the Angel of the Lord addressing him as "a mighty man of valour" (Judg. 6:12). He who prepared a meal for weary Elijah and said to him, "Arise and eat," is the same who prepared a meal for tired disciples on the shore of Galilee and said to them, "Come and dine." Elijah went on the strength of his repast forty days and forty nights (I Kings 19:8), so likewise the disciples until the Ascension, which was forty days later. He is the same yesterday under the old covenant, today under the new, and forever.

"In all their affliction He was afflicted, and the angel of His presence saved them" (Isa. 63:9). Yea, "The angel of the LORD encampeth round about them that fear Him, and delivereth them" (Ps. 34:7). How very constant he is! Apart from Him there is no one that can comfort the soul; without His company nothing can cheer the heart; it is virtually no loss to lose all but this vital Lover.

THE ARK OF THE LORD

> When ye see the ark of the covenant of the LORD your
> God, and the priests the Levites bearing it, then ye shall
> remove from your place, and go after it (Josh. 3:3).

This is one of the most complete and comprehensive types of Christ in the Bible and is worthy of a whole chapter instead of such a brief space which is devoted to it. The ark consisted of a gold-plated casket or chest with two cherubim of carved olive wood overlaid with pure gold covering the mercy seat. Their wings were turned toward the center and their faces looked downward. The model itself expressed the wisdom of the eternal mind, the materials used were emblematic of Christ in manifestation among men, while the presentation of incense and blood demonstrated His perfect character as Mediator for the achieving of reconciliation. The crown of gold upon the ark represented the sovereign authority of Christ in lordship. The mercy seat before which the blood was sprinkled signifies sacrificial death by virtue of lovingkindness, while the content of the ark symbolizes the sufficiency of the administration of Christ in His leadership. Again, the position of the ark in the midst of the camp when the congregation was at rest, the prominence it held in the forefront during advance and the pre-eminence accorded to it during times of access to God in ceremonial functions express Christ in three of His greatest offices.

When John was on Patmos He saw Christ unveiled in the midst of the throne; he also beheld Him tending His flock like a Shepherd and leading by fountains of living waters; but, in addition, he viewed Him in pre-eminence and honor, with the Book in His hand as the only One worthy to open its seals, and with the Bride of the Lamb, glorified in holiness (Rev. 5:6; 7:17; 19:7-8). The ark with its oracle was the governing factor of the nation. It guided the Israelites in their pilgrimage and guarded them against the perils of the way. Christ, likewise, is our guarantee in all three of these experiences. In fact, the beauty, symmetry and utility of the ark remind us in every detail of the manifold ministries of our Redeemer. His was a life independent of circumstances, imperial in conquest, impregnable in constancy and incorruptible in character.

Little wonder that God said to Joshua, when directing attention to the ark, "Go after it" (Josh. 3:3). The eternal Father also draws attention to the great antitype when He says, "This is My beloved Son, in whom I am well pleased; hear ye Him" (Matt. 17:5). Furthermore, the ark was the center of communion and source of commission. "Thou shalt put the mercy seat above upon the ark; and in the ark thou shalt put the testimony that I shall give thee. And there will I meet with thee, and I will commune with thee" (Exod. 25:21-22).

From more than a score of significant experiences the people had in relation to the ark, we record the following four, "The ark of the covenant of the LORD went before them" (Num. 10:33). "He putteth forth His own sheep, He goeth before them" (John 10:4). "Behold, the ark of the covenant of the Lord of all the earth passeth over before you into Jordan . . . the priests that bare the ark of the covenant stood firm . . . in the midst of Jordan" (Josh. 3:11, 17). "The same day . . . the disciples were assembled for fear of the Jews, came Jesus and stood in the midst, and saith unto them, Peace be unto you" (John 20:19). "The ark of the LORD compassed the city . . . the wall fell down flat" (Josh. 6:11, 20). "Thanks be unto God, which always causeth us to triumph in Christ" (II Cor. 2:14). "The weapons of our warfare . . . mighty . . . to the pulling down of strong holds" (II Cor. 10:4). "They brought the ark of God, and set it in the midst of the tent that David had pitched for it" (I Chron. 16:1). "Jesus answered and said unto him, If a man love Me, He will keep My words . . . We will come unto him, and make Our abode with him" (John 14:23).

Not only do we meet with the care of His shepherdhood, the covenant of His suretyship, the conquest in His strength and the companionship of His society as typified in the ark, but also a score of other precious features, which have their parallel in the Christ of the New Testament.

THE ADVOCATE WITH THE FATHER

If any man sin, we have an advocate with the Father,
Jesus Christ the righteous (I John 2:1).

Christ engages in representative consultation on behalf of
His people with a perfect understanding of the divine
character and claims, and a full knowledge of existing needs.
He is unlimited in His personal rights and resources and
unhandicapped by incapacity or inability. In fulfilling this
office of Advocate, Christ upholds the rights of the children of
God, sustains the privileges of sonship and maintains the cause
of every member of the household of faith. "Paraclete" or
"Advocate" is made up of two parts, "para" meaning with, or
alongside, and "klesis," to call; that is, one called alongside.

In the tabernacle of the Old Testament God spake from
between the cherubim which were on the mercy seat of the ark
of the covenant. The two cherubim in their typical teaching
express advocacy. In the New Testament the Spirit of God and
the Son of God are both called advocates. The import is plain.
God the Father has called to His side the Spirit and the Son to
co-operate in the work of mediation and maintenance for the
benefit of His redeemed people. These are tangible tokens of
the lovingkindness of the Lord to reassure our hearts that the
entire work of salvation will be completed.

When a new ocean liner is launched and fitted for passenger
traffic, the contractors supply an ample number of lifeboats,
life buoys and life belts to meet the requirements of all on
board, in case of emergency. A visitor who boarded a large
steamer for the first time asked what all these lifeboats and
buoys and belts were for. He was informed that they were
provided in case the vessel was wrecked. "Oh," said he, "are
they going to wreck this vessel?" "No," said the officer, "they
do not intend to do anything of the kind. They furnish these
helps for the saving of life in case the ship is wrecked."

Let us not conclude that because we have an Advocate with
the Father, Jesus Christ the righteous, we therefore have
license to sin. God forbid. In view of the gracious and generous

provision made for our maintenance, we should gratefully reciprocate our Lord's goodness by abiding in Christ and walking even as He walked (I John 2:6). Christ as our Advocate abides in the beauty of holiness before God continually from generation to generation. He acts in every righteous cause, graciously. He appeals for all who seek spiritual strength and favor, generously. He assures the perfecting of our salvation, gratuitously. He answers for our defects and defaults, grandly. He advocates our access to the throne of grace and acceptance with God on the ground of reconciliation, gloriously.

THE ANCHOR OF HOPE

> Which hope we have as an anchor of the soul, both sure and stedfast, and which entereth into that within the veil (Heb. 6:19).

An anchor is an instrument that holds in security and safety when danger and disaster are threatening. Here again a material figure is taken and its function is personified in living and lasting reality. Messiah is strong and steadfast; therefore the chain of hope is securely fixed to One who never fails. The reason Christ is the Anchor of Hope is that He created a new consciousness which concerns things to come. Anticipation is awakened to look and labor and long for a better country, a brighter city and a more blessed community than can be realized here. Christ Himself is the unanswerable evidence of our ultimate entrance into an immortal society, because as Forerunner, He has for us entered (Heb. 6:20). He has begotten in us a passion for the higher friendship, a belief in the happier fellowship and a faith in the holier family of the household of God, of which he spake as "My Father's house" (John 14:1).

The Apostle Paul declared, "Christ in you, the hope of glory" (Col. 1:27), which hope supplies the energy for endeavor as well as the enlightenment for expectation. Even amid the smoke of strife, the mists of misfortune, the tornado of trial, the billows of blame, the welter of war and tides of trouble, "We have an anchor that keeps the soul, steadfast and sure while the billows roll." Christ as our Anchor is weighty in authority; therefore stable and strong. He is heavy in honor; therefore steadfast and secure. And he is mighty in majesty; therefore supreme and serene.

The entry of Christ on our behalf into the heavenly sanctuary has ratified all the promises of God in perfect righteousness, re-established our relationship to the Father in permanent reconciliation, re-instated our forfeited authority in a prevalent regency, and has registered our redemption from ruin by His pertinent resurrection. Our hope is centered in the divine purpose, which was purposed in Christ before the world began, unto our glory. Christ came to fulfill that purpose; wherefore He is the Anchor of Hope.

THE APOSTLE AND HIGH PRIEST

> Consider the Apostle and High Priest of our profession,
> Christ Jesus (Heb. 3:1).

The word "apostle" means a sent one. "The Father sent the Son to be the Saviour of the world" (I John 4:14), and in so doing sent the most impressive unforgettable character of all history to represent Him. The fact of the nature of the One by whom Christ was sent into the world should suffice for our giving Him a ready welcome and a great reception. The Father is "the Father of lights, with whom is no variableness" (Jas. 1:17); "the Father of spirits," who chastens those He loves (Heb. 12:9); "the Father of mercies," who comforts those in trial (II Cor. 1:3); and "the Father of glory" (Eph. 1:17), who calls us to glory and virtue (II Pet. 1:3). In addition to Christ being the expression of the One who sent Him, He has a very important errand; so that when we consider the motive of His mission, the manifesto of His ministry and the message of His mediation by means of which we have access to the Father, we should most certainly welcome Him with gladness and gratitude.

Christ as the Apostle was specially called and commissioned by the Father as heaven's ambassador to earth. He represents the Father perfectly and heaven in reality. The Father placed in Him absolute confidence and sanctioned full exercise of authority to fulfill the divine purposes, confirm the promises and execute the prerogatives. In the Gospel of John where the word "apostello" occurs seventeen times, a sevenfold identity between Father and Son is disclosed in chapter 5. For example, "As the Father hath life in Himself; so hath He given the Son to have life in Himself" (v.26). "As the Father raiseth up the dead, and quickeneth them; even so the Son quickeneth whom He will" (v.21). Every privilege the Son offers His disciples the Father approves. Every prayer the Son prays, the Father hears (John 11:41-42). Every promise the Son makes, the Father endorses (John 15:26). We, too, have the assurance that the Father responds to all requests asked in the Son's name (John 16:23). Christ affirmed that the motive and method of His life was to do the Father's will, "I came down from heaven, not to do mine own will, but the will of Him that sent Me" (John 6:38). Again He said, "I must work the works of Him that sent Me, while it is day" (John 9:4). The confident claim He made, "I do always those things that please Him," is corroborated by the Father who said, "This is My beloved Son, in whom I am well pleased" (Matt. 3:17).

Christ's representation of the Father in every feature is so appealingly attractive that we may see clearly from the record given how completely He fulfilled His great trust as the Apostle. Mention is made of the bosom of the Father and the bosom of the Son, the love of the Father and the love of the Son, the gift of the Father and the gift of the Son, the glory of the Father and the glory of the Son. These and many more such statements add to the claim, "I and my Father are one" (John 10:30). Christ is the self-revelation of the Eternal in fullness of grace and glory, in faultlessness of judgment and justice, and of faithfulness in purpose and promise.

THE ALTOGETHER LOVELY

> Yea, He is altogether lovely. This is my beloved, and
> this is my friend (S. of Sol. 5:16).

The Song of Solomon is a superlative expression of the
companionship and communion of sacred society as experienced in the seclusion of the stainless sanctuary, described
in Scripture as the Holy of Holies. The delights of fellowship
recounted are wholly foreign to unregenerate lives. The soul in
this case becomes fast-fettered by the bands of eternal love and
initiated into the secret mysteries of a union which is un-
severable. The vibrant springtide of love has dawned, the
fragrant flowerage of affection is redolent and full, the verdant foliage of spiritual grace is unwithering in beauty, the
constant fruitage of goodness is immortally luscious and the
abundant vintage of the untainted wine of joy is age-abiding.
The best Beloved, whose face shines as the sun in His strength,
radiates summerlike charm and contentment in fullness
forever. Bridal affection reciprocates and responds with a
complete description of the Bridegroom's noble character,
combined with the dignity of His personal beauty and royal
integrity (S. of Sol. 5:10-16). The figures of speech that are
used portray every conceivable capacity of virtue, from the
constancy of love, signified in the dove, to sufficiency of
strength pictured in legs like pillars of marble. The imagery
reaches its conclusion with a burst of endowed eloquence,
born of ecstatic endearment, "Yea, He is altogether lovely."
A whole world of wealth is thus packed into five wonderful
words.

THE AMEN

> These things saith the Amen, the faithful and true
> witness, the beginning of the creation of God (Rev.
> 3:14).

In halls of honor and annals of fame, the values of this
unique title, The Amen, are wholly unsurpassed both in

weight of credit and height of merit. This designation might well be the one to which the Redeemer referred when promising the overcomers of Pergamos and Philadelphia a new name because of fidelity to what He termed, "My faith" and "My word" (Rev. 2:13,17; 3:8,12). We may diligently search the chief cities of the nations, examine all the records of the centuries and ransack the literature of continents the world over, but will never find another bearing this name.

The implication of its meaning directs us solely to the Christ, who is the only One that fully comprehended the mind of God, faithfully conformed to the will of God and finally confirmed the Word of God; this He did entirely, completely and perfectly. He did not allow a fraction of any one of the counsels, purposes or desires of the eternal Father to go unrealized. To every divine utterance He said, "So be it," and fulfilled it to the minutest detail, irrespective of what it might cost Him. The Gospel of John records that on twenty-five occasions Christ prefaced the declaration He was about to make with a double "Amen," which is rendered in the Authorized Version, "Verily, verily." In every instance His words which followed expressed truth that man would not have known apart from revelation. In His use of it, He took the word "Amen" out of its usual setting at the end of a sentence or petition, and used it at the beginning. Other than He, no one else had the authority so to do. His action implies, "I, the Amen, say unto thee," (John 3:3); but the word was not actually used as a title until He had rendered obedience even unto death. In Gethsemane, He refused defense against the rabble crowd, saying as He did so that more than 288,000 angels were at His beck and call; "But how then shall the scriptures be fulfilled, that thus it must be?" (Matt. 26:54) He used this number to show that He had more resource in His zero-hour of abject weakness than was available to David at the zenith of his strength (I Chr. 27:1). So He accepted the cup (Matt. 26:42).

As a result of our Lord having said "so be it" to every word of God, one of the great aspects of His ministry was to confirm the promises made to the fathers (Rom. 15:8). Wherefore, today all the promises of God are centered and circled in Him, and we may add our "amen" to the glory of God (II Cor. 1:19-20 R.V.). We affirm again that no one else, anywhere at anytime, always and altogether, said "so be it" to every jot and tittle of the will of God. Because He did, He was able to use this claim when challenged, as the supreme proof of His Sonship, "I came down from heaven, not to do Mine own will, but the will of Him that sent Me" (John 6:38).

THE ALL, AND IN ALL

> Where there is neither Greek nor Jew, circumcision nor uncircumcision, Barbarian, Scythian, bond nor free: but Christ is all, and in all (Col. 3:11).

This title stands at the climax of a forceful summing up in the Colossian Epistle of the famous portrayal of Christ which is made by a twelvefold use of the word "all" in reference to His superior greatness. The description depicts one of the most complete pictures of His superabounding excellence and surpassing eminence found in the Scriptures. After declaring that Christ is the Creator of *all* things, Firstborn of *all*, in precedency of *all*, in the pre-eminence of *all*, the Fullness of *all*, the Reconciler of *all*, the Treasury of *all* wisdom, Head of *all* principality, Nourisher of *all* the body, Forgiver of *all* trespasses and such like, the Spirit gives us this choice compendium, "Christ *all*, and in *all.*" In God's revealed purpose is a new order of things, in relation to which the divisions and distinctions of this old creation are of no account.

Neither Greek nor Jew, circumcision nor uncircumcision, Barbarian, Scythian, bond nor free avail ought. That means that national, ceremonial, racial and social differences hold no brief there, and are alike valueless; for Christ is the All. No room is left for the human or natural elements to intrude; no flesh can glory in His presence. In so far as spiritual relationships are concerned, Christ is the All. All of reconciliation for our acceptance, all of adoption for our association, all of award for our activities, all of admiration for our affection, all of authority for our allegiance, all of affability for our adoration, all of administration for our assurance eternally, and in all else beside, Christ is the All. Not a single relationship is conceivable in the new order of the fullness of times but that in such relationship Christ is the All.

B

The celestial characteristics of Christ supply credentials that support every claim He made, while His distinctive capabilities, which are expressed in work and wisdom, are without compare.

The BEGINNING OF THE CREATION (Rev. 3:14)
>   Christ transcends our human comprehension.

The BRIGHTNESS OF GOD'S GLORY (Heb. 1:3)
>   The resplendence of God in exact resemblance.

The BELOVED SON (Matt. 3:17)
>   The preciousness of perfect affinity in mind and will.

The BRANCH OF RIGHTEOUSNESS (Jer. 33:15)
>   Christ wholly demonstrates the Divine nature.

The BREAD OF GOD (John 6:33)
>   The Sustainer of spiritual vigor and virtue.

The BRIDEGROOM OF THE BRIDE (John 3:29)
>   He is perfectly lovely and lovable perennially.

The BLESSED AND ONLY POTENTATE (I Tim. 6:15)
>   Irresistibly glorious and infinitely lustrous.

The BREAKER, THEIR KING (Mic. 2:13)
>   One who overturns and overthrows evil forever.

The BALM OF GILEAD (Jer. 8:22)
>   The Heavenly specialist in soul-surgery.

The BEAUTY OF HOLINESS (Ps. 96:9)
>   The intrinsic essence of eternal being.

The BUILDER OF THE TEMPLE (Zech. 6:12-13)
>   Christ is wisest and worthiest in workmanship.

The BRIGHT AND MORNING STAR (Rev. 22:16)
>   The Lord is the harbinger of a fadeless daybreak.

JESUS CHRIST

THE SAME YESTERDAY, AND TODAY

The same intimate relationship (Rev. 22:16)
The same imperial authority (Matt. 28:18)
The same inexhaustible wisdom (Col. 2:3)
The same infinite foreknowledge (I Pet. 1:2)
The same immortal loveliness (S. of Sol. 5:16)
The same impregnable righteousness (Dan. 9:24)
The same incorruptible majesty (Rev. 5:12)

AND FOR THE AGES

No cherub can with Him compare
   Nor seraph's flame outshine,
Fairer is He than all the fair
   In holiness divine.

His face outshineth all the host
   Of angels round the throne,
His glory is their constant boast
   Throughout the heavenly zone.

The myriad armies of the blest
   Their Victor hail with glee,
For each one wears the royal crest
   Of Him who set them free.

The Splendor of all heaven above,
   The Head of every rank,
Is Jesus Christ the King of love,
   The One archangels thank.

He made the worlds and still upholds
   The planets, stars and sky,
And future ages shall unfold
   More glorious traits on high.

The honor, majesty and strength,
   Admiring hosts acclaim,
Express the depth and breadth and length
   Of His immortal fame.

I am Alpha and Omega (Rev. 22:13)

Not a single title advanced by Christ concerning Himself in the Word of God, nor any other name by which He is addressed overestimates His transcendent majesty or overstrains His tremendous merit. He is never called by any one of His distinctive designations of honor, without richly deserving the same; and by virtue of His celestial comeliness engraces each with a heavier weight of dignity and a greater degree of excellence in every instance. His suitability as a Governor and His stability as a Guardian are both underived. His durability as a Shepherd and His desirability as a Saviour are not qualifications conferred by any human administration. He is the Lord, "which is, and which was, and which is to come, the Almighty."

Our Lord stated most definitely and clearly during the period of His earthy ministry that His real identity was altogether outside the realm of human observation: "No man knoweth who the Son is, but the Father" (Luke 10:22). This is at once a stately declaration and a startling disclosure. The Word of God expresses the Son and the Son of God expresses the Word. The truth reveals the Son, and the Son reveals the truth. The Scriptures interpret the Son, and the Son interprets the Scriptures. Wisdom unveils the Son and the Son unveils wisdom. The Father declares the Son and the Son declares the Father.

Of the creature it has been aptly said, "Self-commendation is no recommendation"; but that statement does not apply to the Creator. Creature self-commendation is vanity, whereas Creator self-commendation is verity. The love of Christ is the only factor that can teach us Christ's loveliness. Nothing outside of His own personal portrayal of perfection can unveil His own perfectness. The Son Himself must initiate us into a knowledge of His Sonship. None other than the Messiah is able to make manifest Messiahship. The visible image of the invisible God verifies Godhead.

When our exalted and glorified Lord declared to John, "I am Alpha and Omega," He voiced a claim beyond the range

of human comprehension; all we can do is to examine some of
the obvious and surface features of this unfathomable utterance. Christians in general spend far too little time in-
vestigating the incomparable glories of this peerless Christ.
There are many today who have but a poverty-stricken
estimate of Him. We shall now proceed to consider twelve of
the titles beginning with the letter "B."

THE BEGINNING OF THE CREATION

> These things saith the Amen . . . the beginning of the
> creation of God (Rev. 3:14).

A sane simplicity characterizes the statements of Scripture
when the profoundest subjects are declared. This grand title,
the Beginning of the Creation, suddenly ushers us into the
presence of conceptions that far transcend the capacities of
our human comprehension. The purpose Christ had in
making this claim is to remind us of the inscrutable mysteries
and mighty potentialities that lie behind the visible expression
of His presence. Stupendous heights of majesty, profound
secrets of mystery and tremendous powers of mastery
characterized the personal glory He had with the Father
before the world was (John 17:5). The main issue involved in
the title is moral and spiritual; for creation is an instructive
figure directing to the processes of a new creation. "For God
who commanded the light to shine out of darkness hath shined
in our hearts to give the light of the knowledge of the glory of
God in the face of Jesus Christ" (II Cor. 4:6).

In the headship of the person of Christ we see exhibited the
suitability, sovereignty, stability, sufficiency and superiority
essential to the establishing of a new creation. Christ Himself is
the Originator of the mighty powers and processes that
produced the present order of things; He is the Overseer of all
forms and fashions of life, and the objective toward which all
things tend and in which they terminate. Everything visible
and invisible is the purport of His wisdom and the product of
His work; for "without Him was not any thing made that was
made" (John 1:3).

The symbolical and typological teaching takes data from all realms. In the astronomical realm Christ is said to be the Star and Sun; in the animal kingdom He is declared to be the Lion of Judah and the Lamb of God; in the biological world He is titled the Tree of Life and Fountain of Life; in the botanical sphere He is the Rose of Sharon and Lily of the Valleys; in the geological order He is the Rock of Ages and Precious Cornerstone; in the mineral kingdom He is likened to the sardine and jasper stones; and in the philological field He is Alpha and Omega and the Word. Investigate where we will, not a grain of grace, not a mite of mercy, not a spark of sympathy, not an atom of authority, not a trace of truth, not a fraction of faith, not a look of love and not a glow of glory exist without His originating energy.

If we examine the vaster things we must admit that the whole earth is full of His glory, whether this glory be reflected from the sublimity of the sky which is so measureless, the splendors of the stars which are so countless, the shining of the sun which is so exhaustless, the spaciousness of the heavens which are so trackless, the surging of the ocean which is so ceaseless, the spectrum of light which is so matchless, the designs of the snowflakes which are so numberless, the springs of fountains which are so traceless, the superiority of mountains which are so ageless or the fragrance of flowers which are so taintless. These few features in themselves introduce a range of wonders that are indescribable.

Much of this present order is destined to be dissolved (II Pet. 3:11), but the new creation abides forever (Rev. 21:5). Christ is the Establisher of the celestial realms; He inaugurated paradise, with its delights. He is Head of the angelic hosts and the hierarchies of heaven. He designed the stability of a durable dominion and an everlasting kingdom. "Lo these are parts of His ways; and how small a whisper do we hear of Him" (Job 26:14 — A.V. and A.R.V.).

THE BRIGHTNESS OF GOD'S GLORY

Who being the Brightness of His glory (Heb. 1:3).

Here we are introduced to the impenetrable realms of infinite mystery. The declaration which nominates Christ as being "the Brightness of God's glory" introduces a host of new values and virtues. Splendors more spacious and grandeurs more gorgeous continue to unfold with undiminishing freshness and undeclining fullness in every additional unveiling.

Christ is the embodiment of immortal bliss, He is the corona of the everlasting flame, the effulgence of essential light, the burnish of celestial brilliance, the aurora borealis of spiritual magnificence, the radiance of supernal resplendence and the nimbus of heaven's loveliest luster. If the irridescent halo of the ineffable Shekinah that abode on the mercy seat of the tabernacle of old was so awe-inspiring, what are we to say of His eternal excellence, flashing rays of exquisite light from His transcendent countenance to the uttermost bound of heaven's ceaseless domain? (Rev. 1:16; 21:23)

The incomparable splendor of this heavenly majesty is inseparably linked with the tranquil calm of irrevocable triumph which assures the lovingkindness of the Lord God almighty forever and ever (Ps. 36:5-9). "The mercy of the LORD is from everlasting to everlasting upon them that fear Him . . . The LORD hath prepared His throne in the heavens; and His kingdom ruleth over all" (Ps. 103:17, 19). "O LORD my God, Thou art very great; Thou art clothed with honour and majesty . . . who maketh His angels spirits; His ministers a flaming fire" (Ps. 104:1,2,4).

Little wonder that Christ attracts the admiring adoration of the choicest cherubim and the stateliest seraphim, who in robes of whitest radiance worshipfully serve with unswerving fidelity and unceasing felicity. How grandly impressive is the blended beauty, mingled majesty and golden glory of Him who reigns in the dazzling perfectness of spotless purity. His personal presence rivets the attention of myriads of angels, millions of the redeemed and multitudinous hosts, all of whom adore and magnify this ever-blessed One who is the brightness of God's ineffable glory.

Christ had already demonstrated the brightness of God's glory in the beauties of creation, the bounties of revelation and in the blessings of the manifestation. He magnified exceedingly the brightness of uncreated light in the work of redemption, in the plan of salvation, in the goal of reconciliation and in the intrinsic merit of mediation at the right hand of the Majesty in the heavens. Likewise also the stateliness of His saving grace, the delightfulness of His delivering might and the spaciousness of His sanctifying truth combine in reflecting the brightness of God's glory. Our blessed Lord lends luster to the lovingkindness of God, polish to the perfectness of God, burnish to the blessedness of God, beauty to the bountifulness of God, charm to the comeliness of God, glow to the genuineness of God and fragrance to the faithfulness of God. All the luminosity of light and the brilliance of its brightest rays emanate from Him.

THE BELOVED SON

This is My beloved Son, in whom I am well pleased (Matt. 3:17; also 17:5; John 12:28).

On three specific occasions the sublimity of heaven's majestic silence was broken by the audible voice of the Most High bearing witness to the Beloved One. The moment of manifestation was marked by a soul-thrilling testimony which verified an age-long prophetic forecast (Luke 1:32,33; Heb. 1:1,2). The very mission of Messiah also corroborated the distinctive fact of divine Sonship, while the message He brought and the miracles He wrought magnified His heavenly status. The clarity of the Father's witness from the excellent glory should forever dispel any lurking doubt about the dignity and identity of the Son's peerless character. The ring of reality associated with the baptism and transfiguration of Christ provides a replete fountain of refreshment for the renewal of faith perpetually.

Infinite preciousness dwells in the person of the Beloved Son; His matchless beauty of character, His surpassing excellence of nature and His unrivalled display of grace and truth make Him to be altogether pre-eminent in nobility, majesty, dignity and glory. The diadems of divine dominion that adorn His brow glisten and sparkle with scintillating splendor in an environment of immortal loveliness. Our ever-blessed Beloved has no substitute to transplace Him, and no superior to transcend Him, for He fills and floods all heaven with His majestic sweetness. He is nearest in relationship as the Son of man, sweetest in fellowship, dearest in companionship, staunchest in friendship, stateliest in kingship, fairest in lordship and strongest in guardianship, the Victor who is forever resolute and reliable in His purpose and power.

In His position of Sonship, Christ stands pre-eminent with sole claim to all things; also in right of heirship He has no rival; and in honor of proprietorship He ranks highest in the whole of the hierarchies of heaven. Unutterable delights are crowded together in His comely personality. Gracious beyond measure and generous beyond mention is the Son of His love in whom dwelleth all the fullness of Godhead bodily. His brighter glory and broader majesty, combined with His complete range of credentials verify forever that He is essentially God the Son and eternally the Well-beloved.

The Father affirmed His pleasure in the Son's perfections and by use of the pronoun, My, expressed the infinite intensity of affection and intimacy of association that forever bind together in oneness of Creatorhood and Redeemerhood, Kinghood and Shepherdhood, Fatherhood and Saviourhood, Covenanthood and Priesthood, Godhood and Servanthood.

How zealously Christ expressed the Father's likeness by perfectly displaying His mercy! How completely He exhibited the Father's glory, how winsomely He revealed the Father's beauty, how thoroughly He portrayed the Father's sympathy, how fully He unveiled the Father's pity and how graciously He declared the Father's sovereignty! In these features and many more He magnified the Father and glorified His name totally, absolutely and finally.

This masterpiece of representation that so definitely upholds the honor of the Godhead and fully assures the eternal completeness of infinite love is our everlasting consolation and good hope through grace. That same good pleasure which the Father reposes in the Son has made us to be accepted in the Beloved (Eph. 1:6). This is one of the brightest jewels of revealed truth. In spite of our frailties, failures and faults our acceptance knows no hazard because we are accepted in One who is always and altogether acceptable to the Father. Our confidence in approach, our converse with heaven, our communion in the light and our companionship with the Father are all centered in the Beloved. What a precious foundation this revelation furnishes for faith! A worthy factor to encourage our hearts in fervent devotion and to enrich our lives with delight in the Lord, while we express to Him our adoring gratitude!

THE BRANCH OF RIGHTEOUSNESS

In those days, and at that time, will I cause the Branch
of righteousness to grow up unto David (Jer. 33:15).

What glorious names our Lord deservedly wears. For whatsoever title He bears is worth our while dwelling upon. We may be sure that a mine of precious wealth lies concealed beneath. Heaven's everlasting love will be found streaming forth from the perennial fountain revealed in this magnificent prophecy (chs. 30—34). See particularly 31:3, and combine it with the everlasting covenant of 32:40. What a mighty vocation Christ fills as the Branch of Righteousness to vindicate and confirm the Lord's covenant promise and oath made to Abraham, Isaac and Jacob and reaffirmed to David (33:26).

Among more than a score of words rendered "branch" in the Old Testament, this one in particular occurs twelve times, five of which definitely refer to Messiah Himself. From these let us quote: "Behold the man whose name is The BRANCH; and He shall grow up out of His place, and He shall build the temple of the LORD: even He shall build the temple of the LORD; and He shall bear the glory, and shall sit and rule upon His throne; and He shall be a priest upon His throne; and the counsel of peace shall be between them both" (Zech. 6:12,13). Notice the three offices of Prince, Priest and Prophet are indicated here as attached to the Branch. They are also intimated in Jeremiah chapter 33, which deals with three momentous realities: firstly, the bounties of Jehovah's promise, concerning which He is never unmindful (1-14); secondly, the Branch of Jehovah's presence, concerning which He cannot prove unrighteous (15-18); and thirdly, the beneficence of Jehovah's perfectness, in which character He cannot be un- faithful (19-26).

The significance of the title, Branch, is that it expresses a similar nature to Him by whom He is sent and also exhibits an identical life, wholly in accord with the original. Christ came as the Representative of Godhead, to confirm the everlasting covenant. He carried out His supreme assignment to the credit of divine righteousness, to the honor of divine goodness and to the glory of divine faithfulness. Let us also remember that the Branch is unchallengeable in His strength, uncompromising in His might and unconquerable in His power. Each of these qualities he utilized in carrying out the conditions required in the covenant. We should rejoice greatly that the cause of our case was committed to One who is ever constant and abun- dantly able to take care of the commitment entirely and ef- fectively.

The effectual will of God is the great determining factor of the pact. This may be proved by taking notice of the ten "I wills" in the opening section of the chapter. The essential wisdom of God proposed the covenant, while the eternal Word of the Lord, which liveth and abideth forever, completes the contract. The divine authorship and authority of the purpose is affirmed no fewer than fifty-eight times in these four chapters by use of the expression, "thus saith the LORD" and "the word of the LORD came."

Not one of the four great worthies named in the chapter is justified by ceremonies, rites or ordinances, but by the blood of the covenant. The reconciliation Christ achieved was not national, parochial nor circumscribed, but is as surely available to us as it was to Abraham (Rom. 4:23-25). "Even so by the righteousness of one the free gift came upon all men unto justification of life" (Rom. 5:18). The Apostle Peter also assures the same: "Them that have obtained like precious faith with us through the righteousness of God and our Saviour Jesus Christ" (II Pet. 1:1).

For the purpose of assuring us that the Branch of Righteousness, who is the exact replica of Deity, actually came in manifestation to fulfill the terms of the covenant, we find written, "Blessed be the Lord God of Israel; for He hath visited and redeemed His people, and hath raised up an horn of salvation for us in the house of His servant David; as He spake by the mouth of His holy prophets . . . to perform the mercy promised to our fathers, and to remember His Holy covenant; the oath which He sware to our father Abraham . . ." (Luke 1:68-73).

This very One came to Jerusalem in human form, the visible image of the invisible God, the righteous One of the eternal ages. He sat amid the group of His disciples and while taking part in the celebration of the historic Passover festival said, "This cup is the new testament in My blood, which is shed for you" (Luke 22:20). "And I appoint unto you a kingdom, as My Father hath appointed unto Me; that ye may eat and drink at My table in My kindgom, and sit on thrones judging the twelve tribes of Israel" (Luke 22:29-30).

This bond of covenant grace so signally sealed in that solemn hour with the blood of the Only-Begotten can never be broken. The document was entered by El-Shaddai in the celestial council chamber and executed by Emmanuel His Beloved Son. Nowhere in the annals of knowledge is there any record of a worthier agreement being ratified, and in none of the law courts of the centuries was there ever affixed a costlier seal of any covenant, namely "the blood of God" (Acts 20:28).

The very intimation of all this seemed such an impossible suggestion to Jeremiah that he said, "Ah Lord GOD! behold, Thou hast made the heaven and the earth by Thy great power and stretched out arm, and there is nothing too hard for Thee" (Jer. 32:17). Beside indicating the stupendous task to be undertaken, the statement of Jeremiah's also implies that:

No mountain uplifted its majestic head without Him,

No fountain poured forth its crystal waters of its own accord,

No star ever traversed a self-appointed course,

No eagle has yet determined its own powers of flight,

No flower has ever framed its charming beauty,

No forest has designed the secret of its gorgeous foliage,

No valley has planned to produce its verdant vegetation, and

No council of nations established the alternation of day and night.

But He did all of this. Wherefore it is not impossible for Him to establish an everlasting covenant ordered in all things and sure. "There is nothing too hard for Thee," said the prophet; and the Lord changed it to a question, "Behold, I am the LORD, the God of all flesh: is there anything too hard for Me?" (Jer. 32:27)

Furthermore, no power exists that can possibly disannul this compact. If any would seek to qualify to do so it would first be necessary:

To derange the whole fabric of nature's laws and seasons,

To disrupt the processes of day and night (Jer. 33:20),

To dislodge the very ordinances of heaven (33:21),

To determine the number of the sands of the sea shore, innumerable (33:22),

To declare the total of the countless stars (33:22), and

To disprove the reality of the Lord's love for the sons of Jacob (33:26).

However, omniscience and omnipotence reside alone in God; therefore, His immutability remains impregnable and invincible. The Branch, our steadfast Saviour, the Lord Jesus Christ, is characterized by the highest degree of truthfulness, the loftiest measure of faithfulness and supremest standard of righteousness. He is both all-sufficient in His almightiness and all-constant in His abidingness.

He forever dwells on the highest plane of integrity and stands chief in the foremost rank of sincerity; not one syllable of any word He has spoken can fail of realization. His pledge abides, "This cup is the new testament in My blood, which is shed for you." His sacrificial love survives the centuries. His sanctifying truth surmounts all controversial barriers and His throne stands securely steadfast for ever more. No wonder the Apostle Paul exultingly said, "The Son of God, who loved me, and gave Himself for me" (Gal.2:20).

THE BREAD OF GOD

The bread of God is He which cometh down from heaven, and giveth life unto the world (John 6:33).

The context shows that the emancipation from Egypt, which was followed by the supply of manna forty years in the wilderness under Moses, is closely associated with this new claim. During that period of national history, four outstanding experiences are recorded. These experiences relate to the Passover lamb, the Red Sea deliverance, the uplifted serpent and the fording of Jordan. The Apostle John introduces the spiritual significance of these same four features in the opening three chapters of this Gospel. These memorable links with the past, together with Jacob's well (ch. 4), and the pool at the sheep gate (ch. 5), furnish an illuminating background in relation to the far-reaching claim Christ made of being the Bread of God from heaven.

The secret of Israel's sustained strength was linked with the lamb in Egypt, the power at the Red Sea, the manna in the wilderness and the old corn in Canaan. These reflect Christ in His personal holiness at the crucifixion, "a Lamb without spot," His prevailing power in resurrection (John 2:19), His perfect humility in submission, "the Bread which came down from heaven," and His pre-eminent honor in glorification, as the One enthroned high above all principality and power.

The third of these is the subject here, where Christ declared Himself to be the Bread of God. To draw definite attention to the fact of His own manifestation and ordained mission, He refers to the source from whence He came and the sequence of that coming. Bread, in the use we make of it, is bought to nourish those who are alive; but Christ the Bread of God imparts life eternal. John is careful to mention among the essentials of this life, birth, breath and bread, and attributes these in turn to the Triune God. The physical bread we eat is from wheat grown in the ground, from whence our bodies are derived. The calcium, silicon, iodine, iron, phosphates, etc. in an organic form are packed into the wheat in order to build up our strength. In like manner, if we are to become partakers of spiritual life and immortality we must needs eat the Bread of God, which is made up of righteousness, goodness, lovingkindness, graciousness, perfectness, holiness and such like which result in Godlikeness.

Our Lord also claimed, "All that the Father giveth Me shall come to Me" (John 6:37). This is a sure anchorage for faith; for by our coming it is obvious we form part of the Father's gift. The decision to do so leads to a great discovery. "Him that cometh to Me I will in no wise cast out" (v. 37). An eternal mystery is unveiled to everyone that comes. Christ is the true legacy of life; He heartily loves, tenderly calls, sincerely welcomes and gladly receives all who come to Him. No one can have too much of His preciousness, sweetness or loveliness; all He bestows is fresh and fragrant and satisfies forevermore.

THE BRIDEGROOM OF THE BRIDE

He that hath the bride is the bridegroom (John 3:29).

In that bright and beautiful narrative of the book of Ruth, Boaz, the notable kinsman who played the part of restorer and nourisher, also became the beloved bridegroom (Ruth 4:15). When the storm of sorrow and the waves of dire distress which Ruth had encountered died down, a new dawn of radiant splendor broke upon her life, in that she made the soul-stirring discovery that Boaz, the mighty man of wealth, was actually her kinsman and her redeemer. The damsel found in this nobleman a stronger sympathy than she had known before; a sweeter society than she had previously experienced and a dearer relationship of remarkable renown; for Boaz, the mighty, became her very own bridegroom.

The greater reality of the New Testament is reflected in this record; for the Son of God became the Son of man, our near kinsman; so that by identity of life and integrity of love, He might redeem and raise up His Bride, the Church, to share the intimacy and immortality of an eternal union with Himself. The illustrious and illuminating portrayal in the record of Ruth supplies an index to infinite movements that find complete consummation in the marriage of the Lamb (Rev. 19:7).

By virtue of Christ's identifying Himself with human history, God wrought out His great regenerative purpose of salvation. If the celestial One had not entered into the realm of the terrestrial and overcome the infernal power of darkness, mankind would not have had any title to the heritage of light with its infinite glory and incorruptibility.

The Apostle Peter presents this Bridegroom as the perfection of all preciousness, the sum-total of exquisite beauty and majesty; whose life is everlasting, whose love is everabiding and whose endowments in an unwithering inheritance are to be eternally enjoyed. Christ monopolizes loveliness by His heart of lowliness, He multiplies preciousness by His spirit of meekness and He magnifies graciousness by His deeds of kindness. As Bridegroom He is affectionately loving, altogether lovely and always lovable.

The Scriptures disclose a series of illustrious bridegrooms in whose lives are given glimpses in faintest tracery of the tenderness of this eternal Lover. Glimmers of Him are reflected in the first love of Adam for Eve, in the faithful love of Abraham for Sarah, in the fervent love of Isaac for Rebecca, in the fragrant love of Jacob for Rachel, in the fruitful love of Joseph for Asenath, in the faultless love of Boaz for Ruth, and in the fascinating love of Jonathan for David.

The majestic countenance of the heavenly Bridegroom

shines as the sun in its strength, so that the mystery of beauty is manifest at its best and brightest. Through Him the divine luster of lovingkindness beams forth in all the richness of moral goodness. He discharges the highest obligations perfectly. He has always been chivalrous in conflict, valiant in victory, constant in courtesy, loyal in love, thoughtful in tenderness, kingly in kindness and gracious in gentleness. No one is able to find in Him a single trace of failure or the slightest taint of fault or forgetfulness.

How solicitous He is in His care, how steadfast in His love, how sympathetic His heart and how sensitive His Spirit in understanding! Emmanuel displayed infinite affection in coming to earth to select and secure His Bride, the Church, and to present her to Himself without spot or wrinkle or any such blemish. He has designed that His Bride share with Him in joint heirship His celestial home and heritage. Little wonder that the name of this Bridegroom is adored for its unrivalled glory and that His love is admired for its unchanging fidelity.

What a thrill comes to the soul when we anticipate sharing a home with Christ beyond the hills and the horizon. A mansion beyond the mists and the mountains. A possession beyond the plains and the planets. A society beyond the stars and the sky. A dominion beyond the darkness and death. A state of bliss beyond the sun and the shadows. A titled estate beyond the trials and tribulations of time. A paradise beyond the perils and pains of the present era.

> Thou glorious Bridgroom of our hearts
>   Thy present smile a heaven imparts,
> O lift the veil, if veil there be,
>   Let every saint Thy beauties see.

THE BLESSED AND ONLY POTENTATE

Which in His times He shall shew, who is the blessed
and only Potentate, the King of kings, and Lord of lords
(I Tim. 6:15)

The very blessedness of Christ as a Potentate reveals that
personally He is morally suited, judicially qualified and
rightfully entitled to rule and reign forever. Nowhere else in
the Bible is the inaccessible majesty and indescribable glory of
Christ so fully explained and so concisely expressed. He is
described here in His self-existent, self-efficient and self-
effulgent Deity, irresistibly glorious and infinitely lustrous in
His being, wisdom and power. His throne is the origin of
harmony, honor and holiness. He also originated the visible
creation, the virtues of character and the varigations of color.

The foundations of His throne are not shallow and
superficial. The far-reaching suzerainty of His sovereign state
pervades and prevails eternally. The fullness of His celestial
court is not sustained by the contributions of earthly kings.
The faithfulness of His covenant does not depend on the merit
or manpower of nations. The fame of His name is not taken
from the renowned institutions of earth. The flame of His
fervent constancy requires no fuel from human resources for
its maintenance. The final consummation planned was not
determined by the decision of world councils. "The mountains
shall depart, and the hills be removed" (Isa. 54:10), kingdoms
shall wane and empires cease, the earth shall be dissolved and
the sun darkened (Isa. 24:19, 21), the veil shall be removed
and death swallowed up in victory (Isa. 25:7, 8); but Christ
our Potentate, Protector, Provider and Preserver abides
forever. His "years shall not fail" (Heb. 1:12).

How blessed to be able to repair to a Fountain of undying
joy and to drink deeply of its undiminishing bliss (Ps. 16:11).
Here we meet the Supervisor of the whole realm of nature, the
Superintendent of the entire range of providence and the
Sovereign of the abounding riches of grace. His remoteness
antedates all other dignitaries. Immortality is inherent in

Him. The diffusing of light does not diminish His brightness in the slightest degree. The impartation of immortality to His redeemed ones does not impair His own incorruptibility. The ceaseless ministries of His majestic throne do not lessen the grandeur of His personal magnificence. The abundant administrations of His abiding kingdom never abrogate His authority, but amplify it. He never misues or abuses His almighty prerogatives. Throned in matchless majesty, He exercises His immutable will with infinite wisdom and invincible might. And by virtue of the insight of His providence, the foresight of His prescience and the oversight of His omnipresence, He fills the highest stations perfectly and perennially.

The fame of Christ transcends the far-flung renown of the foremost among the famous, His name exceeds the notability of the more noble of this world's nobility, and His claim supersedes the titled claimants of all the centuries. Seeing we have such a Potentate as our Peace-maker, such a Lord as our Life-giver, and such a Justifier as our Joy-bringer, let us ever sing,

> He is my prophet, priest and king
> Who did for me salvation bring,
> And while I live I mean to sing
> Christ for me, Christ for me.

THE BREAKER, THEIR KING

> The Breaker is come up before them . . . and their king shall pass before them, and the LORD on the head of them (Micah 2:13).

Amid a setting of national rebuke and reproof and under conditions in which there was little that existed worthy of the name of government, the Prophet Micah proclaims this bright and brilliant vision of deliverance. The counsellor, their king, had perished (4:9), but a voice of confidence calls attention to the Word of promise, the Spirit of power, and the Ruler in prospect (2:7; 5:2).

In the great pledge of this prophecy the Breaker is to come who brooks no opposition, who overturns oppression, who overrides obduracy and who overthrows all obstacles that stand in the way of permanent peace. The very blackness of the boisterous tempest described forms a suitable background to set forth the finer tints and fairer tones of the brightest rays of blessing ever given. Under the title of The Breaker, Christ appears as the Champion. Chivalrous in conflict, He is the Challenger who without fear assails the encastled foe. Yea, and He is the Conqueror who without fail subdues the rebels and triumphs gloriously. The spiritual values of this section of the prophetic forecast are not only bright with vision but brighter with victory.

He who raised up Gideon the breaker to destroy the yoke of Midianite oppression, who called the mighty Cyrus to break the brazen gates of Babylonian bondage (Isa. 45:2) and who Himself broke the covenant and brotherhood of Israel (Zech. 11:10,14), such an One is the Breaker who in aggressive combat with our great adversary, the Devil, assailed the fortified stronghold of the Devil and disgorged his armor wherein he trusted (Luke 11:21-22; Col. 2:15; Heb. 2:14-15). The victory achieved over the Devil and death is complete.

Christ in His might has also broken down the middle wall of partition that hindered our approach to God, and by Him we now "have access by one Spirit unto the Father" (Eph. 2:14, 18). The dramatic portrayal in Micah's thrilling figure of triumph is associated with certain of the grazing areas in Palestine. When feeding among the thorn bushes, some of the sheep suddenly become startled because they appear to be entirely encircled. Then it is that the strong double-horned ram, with head down, plunges forward and breaks through the thorn barrier and opens a way for the sheep to follow. The rescue of British prisoners from the German deathship *Altmark* supplies another striking illustration of this subject. Until Christ came, underwent crucifixion and thus became the Conqueror, no evidence of victory for humanity over death and no assurance that evil would be vanquished had been established. He has broken the bondage of sin and the bars of death, passed through at the head and led His people to larger life and lasting liberty. He not only breaks the power of cancelled sin but enables each trusting soul to say,

My chains are snapped, the bonds of sin are broken
   And I am free.
Oh, let the triumphs of His grace be spoken,
   Who died for me.

THE BALM OF GILEAD

Is there no balm in Gilead; is there no physician there? why then is not the health of the daughter of my people recovered? (Jer. 8:22)

In heaven the dispensary is hard by the chamber of God. Prayer is the catholicon that commands the attention of heaven and secures the promised healing both physical and spiritual. In the chapter in which James declares that "the effectual fervent prayer of a righteous man availeth much," he says in the context, "the prayer of faith shall save the sick" (Jas. 5:15,16), and that as ministered by the elders of the church. What an encouragement it should be to us, knowing as we do that the source and secret of such sufficiency and sympathy is in our Saviour. An omnipotent influence, one which originates in the bosom of immutable Love, is necessary to effect the change required in most lives. How very exhilarating to the soul is the discovery that in Him is the character of a never-to-be-forgotten Healer.

Jeremiah had told the nation that "the heart is deceitful above all things, and desperately wicked" (Jer. 17:9). The remedies doctors dispense and the deeds lawyers draw up cannot cope with heart maladies of this kind. Church ceremonies with christening and confirmation cannot effect a cure in such cases, and no magical virtue exists in outward forms of external worship to achieve it. Let us beware also of the quackeries that abound in the field of religion.

"Is there no balm in Gilead, is there no physician there?"

Surface symptoms usually have a deep-seated cause, and soul-surgery requires a specialist. One only can be found in all the world, but happily He is omnipresent and available to all. In the alchemy of His divine grace He is able to completely change the heart (Ezek. 36:26). Such surgery results in a new disposition and new devotion, accompanied with new desires. Latent excellencies that few have discovered reside in Christ. He it is that assures lasting emancipation from all heart ailments. In His suitability and sympathy especially, He is a Healer without compare and never changes. The Creator gave to man a delicate intuition toward divine seasons, yet the migratory birds with their instinct are far more responsible than His people (Jer. 8:7). The fourfold use of the word "why" in this chapter is a reflection on man's reluctance to readily receive God's remedies.

THE BEAUTY OF HOLINESS

O worship the Lord in the beauty of holiness: fear before Him, all the earth (Ps. 96:9).

Another of Christ's inherent qualities of character is holiness, which is expressed in perfection of constitution and exhibits completeness in symmetry of virtue, purity of nature and beauty of form. The beauty of holiness constitutes that reality of perfection in character which is expressed in righteousness of conduct in all relationships. This virtue is wholly exemplified in every detail in Christ's desires and doings. His entire activity is inspired by love, infused with truth and immersed in grace. Moses prayed that this beauty of the Lord might be imparted to man (Ps. 90:17). The Lord was not indifferent to this request for He said, "Thy renown went forth among the nations for thy beauty; for it was perfect through My comeliness, which I had put upon thee, saith the Lord God" (Ezek. 16:14). We are pledged to see "the king in His beauty" (Isa. 33:17), and when we see Him we shall be like Him (I John 3:2).

The holy beauty of Christ's character was expressed in the

eloquence of His love so real: "Never man spake like this man" (John 7:46); in the effulgence of light so pure: "Who being the brightness of His glory" (Heb. 1:3); and in the exuberance of life so true: "Anointed . . . with the oil of gladness above Thy fellows" (Heb. 1:9). No one is more desirable in majesty, more affable in dignity, or more amiable in humility than He. How ravished our hearts should be as we reflect on such a Lover. Each branch of art has selected Him as the main subject. This fact indicates that he has motivated the finest poetry, the choicest music and the greatest paintings. His beauties are also signified under the figures of flowers, foliage and fruits; while special features of His loveliness are likened to sparkling dewdrops, feathery snowflakes and precious jewels. Well might we repeat the lines:

> Show me Thy face, one transient gleam
>   Of loveliness divine,
> And I shall never think or dream
>   Of other love save Thine.
> All lesser lights shall lessen quite,
>   All lower glories wane,
> The beautiful of earth shall scarce
>   Seem beautiful again.

THE BUILDER OF THE TEMPLE

> Behold the man whose name is The BRANCH . . . and He shall build the temple of the LORD (Zech. 6:12; also Matt. 16:18; Eph. 2:20, 22).

The temple that was rebuilt by the remnant that returned to Jerusalem from Babylon was but a temporary structure. The five significant features that had been identified with Solomon's temple were withheld. God did not write afresh the tables of the law, nor permit a new ark of the covenant to be made. He withheld from its precincts the divine oracle, the holy fire and also the Shekinah glory. However, He promised a greater Builder and a greater Glory, One who would far surpass in workmanship any of the structures erected by man.

Living stones cut from the quarries of human nature and polished to excellence and perfection by the Spirit of God were to be built by Him into a holy temple in the Lord. The temple Christ builds is constructed from perfected lives, every stone bearing evidence of the character and nature of the Builder Himself. The inter-relationship of redemption is to be centered in eternal fellowship. The dedication of this temple when completed will mark the brightest and most blessed day that ever dawned; for it ushers in a reconstituted kingdom (Zech. 6:13), a reconfirmed victory (14:4) and a regenerated world (14:9). Then we shall rightly adore the Builder for His wisdom, will and work, while angels wonder and worship (Eph. 3:10).

THE BRIGHT AND MORNING STAR

I am the root and the offspring of David, and the bright and morning star (Rev. 22:16).

No one feature of Christ's radiance and renown is more fascinating than the feature of the bright and morning star. At the time of His birth into this world at Bethlehem, a star stood over the house in which the young child lay to direct the sages who had come to worship Him. The scroll of prophecy and the song of the heavenly host had also contributed their witness to His whereabouts. God hung no fresh lamp in the sky to announce the birth of any of the Pharaohs of Egypt, the Caesars of Rome, the Emperors of China, the Rajahs of India, the Caliphs of Mecca, the Sultans of Turkey, the Czars of Russia, the Kaisers of Germany, or the Napoleons of France; but He did place a star to herald the manifestation of this child.

Following such a sign with which to commence His life, Christ was decreed to display a name that is above every name, a priceless name that was to be as ointment poured forth, the very essence of excellence, even like to a paradise of pleasure with its peerless perfection. By virtue of His character he conquered death and ascended to the right hand of the majesty on High. The unutterable glory of His effulgence will break through the mists once more and He will come as the Bright and Morning Star, to be admired and adored by all who believe. Just as conspicuously as the morning star heralds the dawn of each new day and heartens humanity with fresh incentive, so will the blessed Saviour appear to inaugurate His everlasting kingdom. The bright beams of His brilliant light will usher in a day that never decays.

The figure of Christ's exaltation as being far above all heavens is beyond the capacity of human conception, and the fact of His incomparable headship is affirmed as being high above all principalities and powers, might and dominion, and every name that is named not only in this world but in that which is to come. Christ is seated at the right hand of un-rivalled honor in the highest conceivable glory; wherefore we should rejoice exultingly in the stupendous victories He gained as our Leader, our Lover, and our Lord. Yet no theme so stirs the pulses of the soul, or so stimulates the throbbings of the spirit, or so strenghtens the loyalties of service as much as the thrilling thought that He will come again as the Bright and Morning Star.

Not Gabriel or Michael, even though they be drenched in the dignity of ineffable light, not the brightest of the seraphic ranks or the most brilliant designate of the cherubic hosts is next to God, but Man, the Man Christ Jesus (I Tim. 2:5). He is the great and grand Pioneer who opened heaven, the Forerunner who marked the highway, the Breaker who cleared the barriers from the road, Himself the Covenant who assured the children's rights, the firstborn Representative of the family claims, the Head who is joined to the members of His body in an indivisible union, the Firstfruits predicting the homecoming of myriads of His people, the Friend who is preparing a suitable place for us all and the Bright and Morning Star who will usher in the eternal day.

While controversialists are making their observations of this Star of Hope, considering its distance and calculating the magnitude of the constellation to which they believe it belongs, let us show the same attitude as did the wise men of old who sought the direction of its gleam, obeyed the voice of its message and followed the guidance of its light.

The very thought that Christ will come again engenders expectation, encourages earnestness and energizes endeavor. That glad hour of His return will be marked as the occasion of the triumph of trust, the prevailing of patience, the prize of perseverance, the reward of righteousness, the terminus of trial, the end of endurance, the aim of abiding, the heritage of hope and the goal of glory.

Every venture made in His interests will be compensated, all virtue patiently cultivated will be crowned and each victory gained in the service of the King will be celebrated and commemorated with everlasting honor. His appearing assures the project of harvest home (Rev. 14:15), and is the pledge of universal unity being realized (Eph. 1:9-10). Yea, it is then that the problem of war will be solved and the permanence of peace secured (Isa. 9:5-7). That thrice-welcome day will promote the harmony of a new society destined to abide forever.

C

The range and renown of Christ's designations are so dignified by virtue of His essential glory that they surpass in splendor the sum-total of all other names and titles combined.

The CREATOR OF ALL THINGS (Col. 1:16)
Marvel of marvels the Creator submits to crucifixion.
The CORNERSTONE (Isa. 28:16)
Christ fills every position of supreme importance.
The COVENANT TO ESTABLISH (Isa. 49:8)
He ratifies the bond for agreement and association.
The CAPTAIN OF SALVATION (Heb. 2:10)
The celebrated Commandant who conquers death.
The CHIEFEST AMONG TEN THOUSAND (Song of Sol. 5:10)
His winsomeness and wholesomeness are complete.
The COUNSELLOR (Isa. 40:13)
Christ decides and determines eternal decrees.
The COVERT FROM THE TEMPEST (Isa. 32:2)
He controls the wind and commands the storm.
The CHOSEN OF GOD (Luke 23:35)
Choicest in character and comeliest in grace.
The CHRIST OF GOD (John 12:34)
Anointed and acknowledged as above angels.
The CONFESSOR BEFORE PILATE (I Tim. 6:13)
Confession is a major Christian obligation.
The CORN OF WHEAT (John 12:24)
He arose from the zero of shame to the zenith of fame.
The CHIEF SHEPHERD (I Pet. 5:4)
His ceaseless dominion secures deathless glories.

I AND THE FATHER ARE ONE

Christ demonstrated this oneness

> *In the priority of His authorship*
> *In the fidelity of His friendship*
> *In the reliability of His guardianship*
> *In the mastery of His workmanship*
> *In the validity of His heirship*
> *In the identity of His relationship*
> *In the mercy of His mediatorship*
> *In the glory of His creatorship*

THE FATHER OF ETERNITY

THE FATHER OF AGES

Sire of the ages, Author of all life,
  Teacher of the sages, End of mortal strife,
Friendship is Thy glory, mercy Thy delight,
  Ere the hills grew hoary heirship was Thy right.

King of all the kingly, Lord of all in light,
  Meek in heart and lowly, minist'ring in might,
Fairest in Thy beauty, happiest in Thy joy,
  Freest in Thy bounty, gold without alloy.

Loving us so dearly, cherish we Thy grace,
  Standing in Thy merit soon to see Thy face,
Deeply founded pity, Fatherlike Thy care,
  In Thy Home eternal we shall surely share.

Majesty so aptly crowns Thy radiant brow,
  God's Elect most truly serving under vow,
Held by the Almighty, pow'r can never fail,
  Judgment unto vict'ry must on earth prevail.

Jesus and Jehovah harmonize in Thee,
  Judge and Justifier leave no vacancy,
Every office filling, every title Thine,
  Heav'n and earth revere Thee, royalty divine.

I am Alpha and Omega (Rev. 22:13).

Other than our Lord Jesus Christ, no person exists who is in possession of titles and designations beginning with every letter of the alphabet, and no one can truthfully say that His names are merely incidentals casually coined. Every title Christ bears is wisely selected with a set purpose in view, and the profound accumulation of so many such, which rank highest in renown, vouch for that famous unchallengeable declaration made in the Word of God that a name is given to Him, "which is above every name" (Phil. 2:9). No other person, so manifoldly potential in capacity and so many-sided in practical ability, exists.

In majesty of power, in dignity of grace, in beauty of virtue and in eternity of love, Christ is without compare. The expansive orbit of His incorruptible glory never diminishes, the high tide of His imperial authority never recedes and the floodlight of His immortal loveliness never declines. Age cannot palsy His perennial power, nor can the throes of time terminate His thoughtful tenderness. The years cannot compel Him to yield His youthful vigor, nor can the centuries circumscribe His complete control. Duration cannot disintegrate His dominion, nor can millenniums mutilate His matchless majesty or mar His mercy.

What a glorious luster environs His abiding love! What a gorgeous miter engraces His attractive brow! What a gracious scepter engages His almighty hand! What a generous nature expresses His heavenly mind! Yet, withal, the tender touches of His wondrous grace and the silken sympathies of His plenteous mercy are dispensed alike to all; for He is no respecter of persons.

Can any one of us, or all of our capacities combined, ever expect to fully comprehend the Christ of God? How profitable it is to pause a moment and muse on His regal majesty and royal meekness. How edifying it is to think for a while on His replete might and resplendent mercy. How delightful the exercise to contemplate for a time His renowned merit and resourceful ministry. Each of these features surpasses in value and virtue the noblest estimates of the most venerable minds. Appraisers and valuators are altogether out of place in this domain; for the only suitable attitude is reverent worship.

When we attentively consider Him, behold, His bountiful blessings are without boundary, His ocean-wide sufficiency is without trace of a shore, His lustrous lovingkindness is without limit, His care and considerateness are without circumference and the fervor of His fragrant faithfulness is free from all faction or friction, formality or frustration. No artist, musician or poet can set forth Christ to perfection. If we attempt to portray His obvious qualities and virtues by the use of earthly analogies, we must needs utilize thousands of them. Should we venture to present His vocations and virtues even partially, we should require a whole host of types, symbols, memorials, images and figures of speech to depict the range of His renown and to voice the riches of His resource within the visible realm, to say nothing of those functions which still remain unrevealed. No other known Leader is so admirable, no other Ruler is so adaptable, no other Deliverer is so acceptable, no other Helper is so accessible and no other Lover is so adorable as He.

Let us now give our attention to a selection of Christ's titles beginning with the letter "C."

THE CREATOR OF ALL THINGS

> For by Him were all things created, that are in heaven, and that are in earth, visible and invisible, whether they be thrones, or dominions, or principalities, or powers: all things were created by Him, and for Him (Col. 1:16; also John 1:3; Heb. 1:2).

Creation, revelation and incarnation are the three mightiest strands of witness available to us in aiding our minds to comprehend the reality of God. The creation demonstrates His power and appeals to the human reason, the revelation declares His purpose and appeals to the human conscience, while the incarnation displays His presence and appeals to the human heart. In creation, the mighty and the mite, the stupendous and the small, the tremendous and the tiny, the lofty and the lowly contribute their witness to His intricate work and infinite wisdom.

The enormous range of creation is beyond our powers of comprehension. Some worlds are so ponderous that human means of reckoning cannot estimate their size. Stars are so numerous, human calculation cannot determine their number. Distances are so spacious, human standards cannot measure their expanse. Ages are so tremendous, human conception cannot comprehend their dimensions. How impotent and incompetent man appears in the light of such magnitudes! Well did David remark, "What is man, that Thou art mindful of him?" (Ps. 8:4)

Within the bounds of our understanding, when we behold the height of the heavens, the sublimity of the sky, the splendor of the stars, the luster of light and the cosmos of color, we admire with wonder the celestial regions. In the sphere of our physical surroundings we may have our senses engaged and enriched by the symphony of sound, the melody of music, the majesty of mountains, the shimmer of streams, the variegation of valleys, the foliage of forests, the fullness of fountains, the flavors of fruits, the beauty of birds, the glint of gems, the sparkle of sapphires and the gleam of gold.

Even greater values than these await us in the spiritual realm, where we learn to revel in the triumph of truth, the kindness of kinship, the fidelity of friends, the sympathy of souls, the touch of tenderness, the character of constancy, the raiment of righteousness, the joy of justification, the happiness of hope, the pleasure of peace, the luster of love, the vestments of virtue, and in millions more of such marvels which are all marked with the tracery of His fingers and the impress of His creative hands. "Without Him was not any thing made that was made" (John 1:3). Marvel of marvels that such a Dignitary should submit to the cruelty and crime of being crucified and become involved in what was known as "the scandal of the cross."

THE CORNERSTONE

> Therefore thus saith the Lord GOD, Behold, I lay in Zion for a foundation a stone, a tried stone, a precious corner stone, a sure foundation: he that believeth shall not make haste (Isa. 28:16).

If we reflect for a few moments we shall find that every station which is significant, every post that is pre-eminent and every status that is transcendent is filled by Christ. The extensive range and exceeding richness of the symbolism employed to set Him forth is adapted from every vocational, professional, cultural and official sphere.

In work of construction one of the most conspicuous features is the cornerstone, and it is usually inscribed with the name of some dignitary and accompanied with a date or brief description of the purpose for which the building was erected. "He that built [or established] all things is God" (Heb. 3:4). "The stone which the builders rejected is become the head of the corner," quoted Christ (Mark 12:10). Isaiah indicates the definite intent God had in mind when laying this precious Cornerstone in the place of greatest prominence. The prophet presents Messiah as the only center for rest and citadel of refuge from divine judgment (Isaiah 28:12). All other implied hiding places for protection, including death itself, are described as being too short, too narrow and too unstable to secure any man against the overflowing scourge of justice. Christ is the sole refuge that is definitely adequate and appropriately near us to which we may turn in the hour of decision.

> God will not justice twice demand,
> First at my bleeding Surety's hand
> And then again at mine.

THE COVENANT TO ESTABLISH

> Thus saith the LORD, In an acceptable time have I heard Thee, and in a day of salvation have I helped Thee; and I will preserve Thee, and give Thee for a covenant of the people, to establish the earth, to cause to inherit the desolate heritages (Isa. 49:8).

According to our Lord's expressed desire and determined design, the harmony of heaven is yet to be established in the earth and will be hailed universally by all humanity. With this in view, He taught His disciples to pray, "Thy kingdom come. Thy will be done in earth, as it is in heaven." He came to establish a covenant with the earth. Covenants are usually compacts of mutual agreement which bind the parties concerned to some specified course of action or behavior. God has by no means disconnected the things of earth from His eternal interests; He revealed to Jacob at Bethel that a vital link of communication existed between earth and heaven and that a definite objective was planned for mankind.

"God was in Christ" and has determined His method of dealing with man through Christ as Mediator. The covenant includes redemption, reconciliation, regeneration and revelation. Christ is the Redeemer, Reconciler, Regenerator and Revealer; for He Himself is the Covenant, He is the One who answers for sin, ascends to the Father, assures the Holy Spirit, appeals for our supplies and achieves our acceptance in Himself, the Beloved. In view of what He is, He far exceeds all that He performs for us. Our main desire should be directed to knowing Him personally and intimately, for a whole Christ is ours.

The bounty He confers is not to be compared with the beauty of His character. The blessings He bestows are not as precious as His delightful person. The legacies he bequeaths are not as lustrous as His heart of love. The gifts of His generosity are not as great as the glory of His own goodness. Even the ministry of His mediation is by far superseded by the Master Himself. In Him all covenant promises, privileges and possessions in connection with the eternal inheritance are confirmed, while present-day protection, provision and peace are guaranteed. A whole Christ constitutes our portion in all the fullness of His stainless life, faultless love and fadeless light. What would believers do without the covenant blessings which Christ has bestowed so bountifully? Yea, rather, what would they do without the Blesser Himself, who is actually the covenant (see Isa. 42:6)?

We should carefully consider what a mighty thing a covenant can be when it is a bond which holds the almighty God to His pledge. He will never tarnish His honor nor disgrace His truthfulness by disregarding His sacred and solemn contract. The validity of a human charter usually depends on the character of the signature and authority of the seal appended to it. What then shall we say of this covenant which has been ratified by the blood of Christ, and which bears the insignia of that glorious Name which is a memorial throughout all generations? We might well say with David, "Whom have I in heaven but Thee? And there is none upon earth that I desire beside Thee" (Ps. 73:25).

THE CAPTAIN OF SALVATION

> For it became Him, for whom are all things, and by whom are all things, in bringing many sons unto glory, to make the captain of their salvation perfect through sufferings (Heb. 2:10).

Christ is not only the Author of Salvation as we saw earlier; He is likewise Captain, to lead His people in an aggressive campaign against the forces of unrighteousness. How suggestive it is that "Joshua" in the Old Testament means the salvation of Jehovah; and the book which bears Joshua's name illustrates the subject in hand. At the very beginning of his career of conquest in Canaan, Joshua observed a man with drawn sword standing over against him. Soldierlike, he immediately approached and said, "Art thou for us, or for our adversaries?" The reply came, "Nay; but as captain of the host of the Lord am I now come" (Josh. 5:13,14). Joshua fell on his face and worshipped, and instantly asked his superior Commander for orders. Then came the august demand,

"Loose thy shoe from off thy foot." (Notice the two words "shoe" and "foot" are in the singular number. The law had been given previously that when an Israelite was incapable of performing a social function or national duty, one shoe was to be removed. See Deut. 25:5-10; Ruth 4:7-8).

Joshua was called upon to acknowledge his incompetence to lead a nation to victory, and he promptly did so (Josh. 5:15). No one other than Christ has the capacity and capability of saving the soul; therefore He is the sole Captain and Commander in Chief in the field of battle and is perfectly able to assail the citadel of the enemy and deliver the captives. How quickly the battlements of Jericho crumbled when Joshua yielded to the celestial Commandant! Let us also take heed, for the Captain of Salvation still stands with drawn sword (Rev. 2:12). We need His presence and presidency every passing hour if we would prevail over the opposing powers that assail us; for He has said, "Without Me ye can do nothing" (John 15:5).

Christ is the Captain who is always virtuous in chivalrous conduct, ever vigorous in His consistent consecration and continually victorous in His truceless warfare. We see combined in the perfect stature of His royal nature the gold of genuine greatness, the silver of sterling sympathy, the brass of boldest bravery and the iron of infinite imperiality. No room is left for man's carnal judgment or foolish reasoning to intrude or to intervene in any campaign this Commander conducts.

THE CHIEFEST AMONG TEN THOUSAND

My beloved is white and ruddy, the chiefest among ten thousand (S. of Sol. 5:10).

When King David, in an hour of national emergency, determined to lead his army in battle against Absalom and his rebels, his own loyal followers vigorously protested, saying, "Thou shalt not go forth . . . thou art worth ten thousand of us" (II Sam. 81:3). If it were possible for us to muster a group of ten thousand worthies, including the greatest leaders, potentates, celebrities, principalities, governors, dignitaries, supervisors, legislators, presidents, emperors, kings, princes, lords and rulers, we should find that the one of chiefest dignity, noblest rank and fairest countenance of all would be our blessed Lord and beloved Saviour, Jesus Christ (Eph. 1:21).

> No mortal can with Him compare,
>   Among the sons of men,
> Fairer is He than all the fair
>   That fill the heavenly train.

Christ is more winsome than any language can possibly convey. The tongues of men and of angels falter when attempting to describe the transporting sight of a transfigured Saviour, such as overwhelmed the three disciples on the mount. We need to be stirred to a state of rapture, fired with a burning heart to a degree of holy ecstasy, so that our souls can mount up with wings as eagles to behold in the highest and holiest the Chiefest among Ten Thousand. Lord, reveal Thyself that we may behold Thy beauty in the sanctuary with its dignity and glory, until our enraptured hearts burst forth into songs of adoring gratitude, and we bless Thy holy Name in ceaseless praise.

Christ is chiefest in the comeliness of His personality, in the winsomeness of His character, in the sweetness of His disposition and in the loveliness of His divine nature. No one is more acceptable in graciousness of manner, or more affable in affectionate kindness than this blessed and only potentate, the King of kings and Lord of lords. Our Superior is also chiefest in praise, power and perfection; for He is the purest of the holy, the strongest of the mighty and the brightest of the resplendent. He is chiefest as Creator of adoring angels, as Possessor of amazing worlds, as Maker of astounding stars and as Designer of abiding glories.

What then shall we render to the Lord for His benefits and blessings? Shall we bring an offering of metal or money, fruits or fabrics, gems or gifts? Why, all such things are perishables. What does He regard most from His redeemed ones? The heart's love and loyalty, the mind's admiration and worship and the will's submission with self-abnegating service. These attitudes and activities are of more value to Him than all the mass of material things we may bring.

The more we contemplate Him the loftier and lovelier He becomes, until His personal attributes expand into a whole world of worthiness, a paradise of perfections, a constellation of comeliness and a galaxy of glory. Amazing thought, that He should condescend to bear our sin, our shame and our dishonor (Ps. 69:19).

THE COUNSELLOR

> Who hath directed the Spirit of the LORD, or being His counsellor hath taught Him? With whom took He counsel, and who instructed Him, and taught Him in the path of judgment, and taught Him knowledge, and shewed to Him the way of understanding? (Isa. 40:13-14)

Whenever the word "counsellor" is used in Scripture the fact of creation stands in close proximity (see Isa. 40:26; also Rom. 11:34,36). Whatever the Counsellor determines is done and none can revoke His decision or rescind His decree. All of the divine ordinances pertaining to the sun, stars, seas and seasons are controlled and coordinated by the counsel of his omnipotence. Christ is both Generator and Governor of all the great features and forces of the entire universe. He is the Counsellor who asked the Patriarch Job if he were competent enough to bind the sweet influences of Pleiades or to loose the bands of Orion (Job 38:31). According to astronomical estimates Pleiades is three thousand billion miles away from the sun and yet this constellation controls the whole of our solar system. Whose counsel, other than His, is authoritative enough to ordain ordinances that will operate such majestic constellations over the range of these gigantic distances with meticulous precision?

This same Counsellor communicated to the prophets a clear, concise account of future events, which we call prophecy. He commissioned Isaiah to issue a challenge to human counsellors to forecast the future or to foreordain things to come. The prophet returned with the report that he failed to find a single one who could do it (Isa. 41:22,23,28). In contrast with this impotence stands the divine omnipotence, "Declaring the end from the beginning, and from ancient times the things not yet done, saying, My counsel shall stand, and I will do all my pleasure . . . I have purposed, I will also do it" (Isa. 46:10,11). Christ is the only Counsellor who has communicated to man a complete record of the ages from the commencement to the consummation.

Isaiah was also told to announce the names of collaborators, if there were any, with whom Christ took counsel in order to ask for advice and aid in His administration; but Isaiah could not submit one solitary name (Isa. 40:13,14). If we are incapable of coining or changing a single decree in His divine purpose, or of constructing or correcting one solitary sentence of His revealed will; if we are incompetent to create and control either planet or comet or determine its orbit, why not acknowledge and adore Him as the wonderful Counsellor, and wholly yield our lives to His will, which we may prove to be good, acceptable and perfect? (Compare Rom. 11:33-36 with Rom. 12:1,2.)

No one else possesses a greater and fuller claim or better title than Christ to counsel His redeemed people. He is altogether entitled to do so because He is the all-wise Creator and also because He submitted to a cruel cross in order to redeem and reconcile. He is abundantly entitled to counsel us because He is the only One who conquered death and the Devil and defeated the powers of darkness. He is admirably entitled to counsel us because as Heir of all things He alone bears the qualifications to confer heirship; He alone maintains our right to inherit an incorruptible estate by His continually making intercession for us. He is assuredly entitled to counsel us because of His care under all conditions; He has secured the cancellation of our sins and comforts us in times of sorrow. "Thou wilt guide me with thy counsel, and afterward receive me to glory" (Ps. 73:24).

THE COVERT FROM THE TEMPEST

Behold a king shall reign in righteousness, and princes shall rule in judgment. And a man shall be an hiding place from the wind, and a covert from the tempest; as rivers of water in a dry place, as the shadow of a great rock in a weary land (Isa. 32:1).

Very few coverings are capable of resisting a boisterous wind, but Christ demonstrated during His earthly ministry that He was completely able to control the wind and command the storm (Matt. 8:26; 14:32). No one else is in possession of credentials to handle and harness this invisible force. We are fully assured that the unseen powers of evil suggested in this passage, which are so real, cannot disturb those who have realized that Christ is the Covert from the Tempest. His omnipotence outvies and overthrows all opposition that would otherwise overwhelm us. Such a blessing, under the circumstances described, is in the highest conceivable degree most desirable. How wonderfully Christ adapts Himself to meet our needs under every exigency of change and challenge. What considerateness that He should condescend to become to us a shadow in the sultry heat and a river to refresh in the drought and dearth of summer.

Metaphors are multiplied to reflect as in a mirror the glory of the Lord, and His incalculable grace and love. These graphically descriptive words are not only applicable to Christ, but He is the only One in His adorable person who can fulfill all the functions that are indicated. The first of the metaphors is that of a king valiant in virtue, whose royalty is unquestionable, whose rule is unchallengeable and whose righteousness is undeniable. The assurance of complete preservation is based on the resolute steadfastness of the reign which can neither be restricted nor restrained. The throne is sufficiently established to ensure stability and confidence in the ruler who is never misplaced.

Notice particularly that the reigning majesty is not in some remote dominion to make him unavailable and inaccessible, for the figure changes and we are immediately told, "A man shall be an hiding place from the wind." This speaks of sympathetic security as based on a gracious affinity; the ruler is formidable as a monarch but friendly as man. He is very notable but very nigh, his regal imperiality is linked with real identity. Christ the Son of the Most High has a notable kingship, but as Son of Man He holds a near kinship.

Such an One is our Covert from the tempest, a Deliverer in times of trouble and a Defender in the test of trial, able to safeguard under every conceivable condition. The rare combination of efficient capacities resident in Him declares that He is equally complete and competent in all circumstances of conflict or comfort, quest or quiet, rigor or rest. He holds us in His strong hand tenaciously but tenderly in the night and height of the ranging tempest, assuring us that all is well. The foundations of the stronghold are fixed in the bastions of everlasting righteousness and the girders are tempered with the intensest love of the infinitely holy One.

We can also be at rest as regards renewal and refreshment. He is "as rivers of water in a dry place." This figure indicates a repleteness of resource that cannot be reckoned or measured, which means enlightenment for the mind, enrichment for the heart and an enlargement for the life that exceeds all estimates. Rivers, rivers, eternally flowing, forever clear and full; and the flavors also of His favors are always fresh. Rivers are fit emblems for the exceeding excellence of His enduring blessedness and blessing. What invaluable riches of resources are reflected here, both trackless in quantity and traceless in quality. Do we fear He will scarcely have enough to nourish all the redeemed ones? Be not perturbed; everyone shall flourish beside the living fountains of waters (Rev. 7:17). The bountiful springs and plentiful supply in beautiful surroundings will suffice and satisfy eternally. There are no bounds to the abundances of Christ, no shores to His sufficiencies, no bars to His benefits and no borders to His blessings. Where He reigns, the dimensions of depth and degree cannot be defined, the light never wanes, the leaf never withers, the love never wavers and the life never wastes away. How grandly He guided the pen of this prophet to reveal the numerous gracious features of our Saviour's manifold ministry.

Isaiah concludes the paragraph by stating that He is "as the shadow of a great rock in a weary land." The merits of such majestic strength cannot be measured by a mean and miserly disposition. For the mind to be capable of calculating and comprehending the multiform care Christ exercises towards those He holds closest and dearest, we need the strengthening by His Spirit in the inner man (Eph. 3:16). Who is qualified to estimate the impregnability of this Rock of Ages (Isa. 26:4)? Who is going to appraise the inestimable value of the shadow which is cast to shield and shade the soul from the sirocco of burning lust or the glare of gaudy temptation? Who, may we ask, is prepared to nominate a price for the indispensable integrity which is indicated in the steadfastness of so formidable a bastion?

THE CHOSEN OF GOD

> And the people stood beholding. And the rulers also with them derided him, saying, He saved others; let Him save himself, if He be Christ, the chosen of God (Luke 23:35). My servant whom I have chosen (Isa. 43:10).

Christ is assuredly preferred above all by the very heart of the eternal God; for He is distinguished beyond all others in the heaven of glory and is pre-eminently desirable because of His holiness in grace and goodness. This same Chosen of God is the One in whom we have been chosen for eternal companionship. What an honor! (John 15:16) To be thus initiated into such an association is one of the inestimable privileges of our relationship in the Beloved. Christ is God's Elect, the stateliest of the sanctified, in whom the Father's soul delighteth because He can never fail in fulfilling the eternal purpose and glorifies the immortal Majesty in all things (Isa.42:1).

Christ is the Chosen of God because of His comely character, because of His charming countenance, because of His changeless constancy, because of His crowning capability and by virtue of His complete conformity in discharging every obligation to do the will and work of God. What an object for our heart's affection is this unmatched, unequalled, unexcelled chosen of God! We should take particular notice of the sacred simplicity, stately sublimity and the sterling sincerity that characterized all His actions.

The affection of the Father had a perfect object in His Chosen and therefore He had no need to choose us; but we are nevertheless chosen in Him who is the Chosen of God, which reality is according to the good pleasure of His will. God is inconceivably pleased with His Chosen, because His and God's blended interests form the essence of mutual harmony and their agreement is the very soul of affectionate accord and abounding amity. Herein we approach the fathomless mystery of Godhead and comprehend in some small degree the perfect consciousness of prevailing calm which abides the ages.

All resources are revealed in a Person, whether they be the realities of goodness, the riches of grace, the rays of glory or the rarest of gifts. All reach us through the Chosen of God. No spiritual blessing comes to us by blind chance but by divine choice. We are chosen in Him before the foundation of the world, we are called in Him, justified in Him and blessed in Him with all spiritual blessings (Eph. 1:3-7). These stupendous verities magnify the amazing mystery of reconciliation which was wrought by One infinitely blessed. Who could doubt acceptance with God in One so acceptable? No one who selects the Saviour as Surety and Substitute will ever regret the step taken. God rests in Him, in Him I rest, even "My servant whom I have chosen" (Isa. 43:10).

THE CHRIST OF GOD

> The people answered Him, We have heard out of the
> law that Christ abideth for ever (John 12:34).
> Simon Peter answered and said, Thou art the Christ,
> the Son of the living God (Matt. 16:16).

The Christ of God is the hope of glory, for He is the glory of
our hope. The title means the anointed One, appointed of
God to guard and guide the redeemed host. The rare qualities
of the Christ ravish the heart, renew the mind and refresh the
soul to the utmost repleteness of satisfaction, until we become
complete in Him. Christ in His fairness incorporates the
fullness and faithfulness of Godhead bodily. He is the
Fountain of ceaseless freshness and compassionate forgiveness;
He is also the Foundation of constant friendship and consistent
fellowship. The Messiah is eminently gracious, extremely
precious and exceptionally glorious. He is the Judge of the
brutish, but the Justifier of the believer. His anointing attests
His kingship and affirms His priesthood, by means of which
offices He regains all authority from the adversary and reigns
unabatingly through the ages.

Christ is the supreme One in a special sense: He is indivisible
in purpose, irresistible in integrity and invincible in strength.
His ministry was governed by one superior motive. He was ever
in perfect harmony with the mind of heaven, engrossed and
enthralled by the Father's will. His whole being was girded
with glorious strength, He was anointed by almighty
authority, robed in resolute righteousness and went into battle
against the foe fully armed with the accouterments of moral
valor and spiritual virtue. The enemy's glamorous reserves of
angels, principalities and powers were amassed in clamorous
array to defeat Him. At the central arena of the conflict stood
a brutal cross, the emblem of shame and contempt to which
wicked hands had nailed Him. The amalgamated forces of
evil were enlisted against Him, the power of death was in the
hand of the enemy, the whole weight of infernal hatred,
diabolical malice and fiendish enmity confronted Him in that
crucial hour; but His armor was impenetrable. He triumphed

gloriously and made a full exposure of the great adversary (Col. 2:15), a conquest which entitled Christ to hurl the deceiver from the battlements on high (John 12:31). This Christ is our Conqueror valiant in victory. His eternal triumph is attended with resurrection mastery, ascension glory and coronation majesty. The Devil is thoroughly defeated and completely vanquished.

THE CONFESSOR BEFORE PILATE

> I give thee charge in the sight of God, who quickeneth all things, and before Christ Jesus, who before Pontius Pilate witnessed a good confession; that thou keep this commandment without spot, unrebukable, until the appearing of our Lord Jesus Christ (I Tim. 6:13).

Our Lord was brought before Pilate as One who had made a claim to kingship. Standing as a prisoner, condemned, and without any visible palace, such a claim seemed preposterous. Altogether devoid of stately robes and courtly attendants and minus even crown or scepter, He nevertheless affirmed emphatically, "I am a king," "My kingdom is not of this world." Christ disclaimed the vainglory of a temporal diadem, but He did not deny His claim to crown rights of a nobler royalty than that shared by earthly rulers. Although He was betrayed, accused and mocked, yet with unflinching, undaunted courage He remained uncowed and uncompromising before the Roman regent; and by patient courtesy and perfect control, He vindicated the essential truthfulness of His superior sovereignty. Remember that within the confines of His Deity this Confessor dwells in light which no one can approach unto and which no man hath seen nor can see (I Tim. 6:16).

If He deemed it wise and worthwhile to acknowledge His claim and right, soldiers of the Cross should learn a lesson from their Captain. "Though it doth not appear what we shall be," let us be prepared to bear witness to the truth of the King's return. Paul the aged, as he termed himself, had borne the burden and brunt of battle and was seeking a successor for his trusteeship. He admonishes Timothy to stick to his business and stand by His witness while focusing faith on the great File-leader. Confession of our faith in the truth of God is our solemn obligation and responsibility, likewise also confession of faith in Christ (John 18:37; Rom. 10;9,10). Jesus Christ as a Confessor of truth is now glorified, and this fact should stimulate all of us to faithfulness in witness. The Saviour testified concerning His kingdom of spiritual truth, of sovereign power, of steadfast righteousness and of sanctified citizenship. Said He, "For this cause came I into the world that I should bear witness unto the truth" (John 18:37). Is this not the very cause and core of the campaign in which we are enlisted? Let us see to it, while our comrades march to face the foe, while our fighting forces shout in the field, and while our friends pray for us in all fidelity, that we often and openly commend and confess Him while the opportunity is ours.

THE CORN OF WHEAT

Verily, verily, I say unto you, Except a corn of wheat fall into the ground and die, it abideth alone: but if it die, it bringeth forth much fruit (John 12:24).

Death, the experience which is fatal to most folk in destroying their influence, was to become the most forceful factor in promoting forever the prestige of Christ. The extent to which memory exercises its influence over the living is definitely limited. If a leader's work is to develop extensively, it is not thought desirable that He should die in the prime of life. However, in this case it was otherwise. Because Christ as the Corn of Wheat fell into the ground and died, He became Administrator of the mightiest authority ever wielded over the minds of millions. He encountered the most odious instrument of death in the form of a crude Roman gibbet, but by virtue of that shameful death He overpowered the cruelest foe, the Devil, and overcame the strongest enemy, Death. Christ's greatest honor arises from His deepest humiliation. He ascended from the zero of shame to the zenith of sovereignty.

Christ, crucified, has an irresistible attractiveness and has become the center to which all contrite hearts are drawn. His own application of this figure makes it crystal clear, "And, I, if I be lifted up from the earth, will draw all unto Me. This He said, signifying what death He should die" (John 12:32, 33). Here infinite love is revealed stooping to die; immortal glory condescends to bear the blame of guilt; intrinsic holiness submits to being made sin for us that we may be made the righteousness of God in Him. When His body was buried in the tomb, it was not as the Romans considered it, a corpse, but what prophecy foretold, a seed; therefore resurrection was assured (Acts 2:27, 28). Likewise the sayings of the Saviour when He was dying survive death and serve to stimulate all successive generations.

THE CHIEF SHEPHERD

And when the chief Shepherd shall appear, ye shall
receive a crown of glory that fadeth not away (I Pet. 5:4).

One of our highest glories on the highland of heaven will be the privilege of honoring our Chief Shepherd, the Lord Himself. How singular is this superior station He fills, which was secured by the supreme sacrifice He made in laying down His life for the sheep. He submitted to severe suffering for the sake of His flock and secured salvation and liberty at great cost and care. He surpassed the sympathy of all other shepherds combined, and steadfastly determined to safeguard the life of His people forever (John 10:29). In this capacity as Chief Shepherd He has pledged to gather His own and share with them the fadeless laurels of His greatest triumph.

No withering wreaths adorn His immortal brows, but many diadems (Rev. 19:11). His distinguished trophies know nothing of tarnish or decay. And He pledges to bestow similar honors of consequence upon His undershepherds, both juniors and seniors. Such honors are described as being, "a crown of glory which fadeth not away." The Chief Shepherd is calling His sheep to eternal glory. Only One who is in possession of deathless glories Himself could promise fadeless rewards in an endless kingdom. Such treasures are not like the transient tinsel this world offers but are heavy with holy honor and weighted with immortal virtue. "Fear not, little flock; for it is your Father's good pleasure to give you the kingdom" (Luke 12:32).

The final portrayal of Christ's leadership of His sheep and lordship of His people given in the Scripture is that of leading His fair and formidable flock by living fountains of water in the thornless fields of a pleasurable paradise, where the tombless landscape of Emmanuel's land is eternally free from the grief of graves, and where the tearless heritage of abiding bliss abounds with everlasting joy (Rev. 7:17).

The Caretaker of this great concourse of emancipated peoples is the Lamb. How very significant that this title should occur here. The fact reveals that the King in authority is the kinsman Associate, the Lord in superiority is the Lamb in sympathy, the Mediator in majesty is the Man in mercy, the Chief in command is the Comrade in companionship and the Sovereign in government is the Shepherd in guidance. This forecast of the Lamb being the foremost Leader indicates that the flock partakes of the same divine nature as the Chief Shepherd. This means similarity of sanctity; for the multitudes have washed their robes and made them white in the blood of the Lamb (Rev. 7:14). Not the smallest speck or slightest stain mars the resplendence of a single robe. But it also indicates likeness in the identity of immortality; for in pitching His tent among our tents, He brought life and immortality to light through the Gospel (II Tim. 1:10). Here also is portrayed sameness in the harmony of humility. The Lamb is not only the Lover of the sheep; He liberated them from the bondage of death and became the Leader of the new society. All reciprocate His love because He first loved and laid down His life for the sheep (John 10:11,15).

In this realm He has prepared, the sheep neither hunger nor thirst; for the celestial benefits and blessings satiate the souls of His redeemed. His resources are replete and His provision complete. The sun is no longer a menace to the comfort and welfare of the flock. Perfect harmony exists between the heavenly hierarchy and the host of the Lord. Furthermore, He wipes away all tears. Even the choicest and saintliest have borne the heaviest physical burdens, sickness and pain, and the scythe of death spares not the choicest friends that are cherished most.

These descriptive figures of ultimate issues furnish a wonderful picture of complete contentment. The charm and calm of the rest He gives is not endangered by harm of any kind. These cherished hosts are satisfied with His wondrous grace, gratified with His precious gifts and beautified with His spacious glory. The entire company enjoys the grace and employs the gifts to promote the praise of His goodness and glory. No unsatisfied desires remain, no unsuited delights exist and no unsecured dwellers reside in Emmanuel's land. The gifts bestowed are not too great for the moral state, the light beams diffused are not too bright for the spiritual sight and the current news broadcast brings no fear or tear, but continual cheer to the communal ear of the perfect society.

D

These titles are famous for their unprecedented splendor and unsurpassed grandeur. Christ exceeds the renown and royalty of all earthly celebrities and potentates.

The DAYSPRING FROM ON HIGH (Luke 1:78)
    The One who floods the world with Divine light.
The DAYSMAN BETWIXT US (Job 9:33)
    The Reconciler to God of the alienated.
The DESIRE OF ALL NATIONS (Hag. 2:7)
    The sole Mediator between God and man.
The DELIVERER OF ZION (Joel 2:32)
    Almighty in His ability to make free.
The DEW OF ISRAEL (Hos. 14:5)
    His beauty and glory are everlastingly fresh.
The DISCERNER OF THE HEART (Heb. 4:12)
    The most keen in penetrating discernment.
The DEFENDER AND REFUGE (Ps. 94:22)
    Who vindicates and safeguards forever.
The DECLARER OF THE NAME (John 17:26)
    The pinnacle of our Lord's ministry.
The DOOR OF THE SHEEP (John 10:7)
    Christ, the only access to the Father.
The DIVIDER OF DAY AND NIGHT (Gen. 1:4)
    The great Discriminator between good and evil.
The DAYSTAR TO ARISE (II Pet. 1:19)
    The Heavenly sign of eternal daybreak.
The DISSOLVER OF ALL THINGS (II Pet. 3:11)
    He consumes the old and creates the new.

THE SON OF MAN CAME

TO SEEK AND TO SAVE

Speaking as never man spake,
  He declared the Father's decrees and desires
Seeking as never man sought,
  He found the lost and lone and saved them
Teaching as never man taught,
  He represented and rehearsed unseen realities
Working as never man wrought,
  He built the bulwarks of the eternal city
Buying as never man bought,
  He purchased at infinite cost the entire field
Fighting as never man fought,
  He foiled the enemy and frustrated his designs
Bringing as never man brought,
  He bestowed on the Church God's bounteous gifts.

TEACH ME, O TEACH ME!

Teach me but Christ, all wisdom you bestow,
  Teach me all else I less than nothing know.
Teach me His mercy and His tender care,
  Transport me Heav'nward for He dwelleth there.

Tell me the hist'ry of His earthly life,
  Show me His vict'ries gained in deadly strife.
Make clear the cross whereon my Saviour died,
  Nought really matters save Him Crucified.

Teach me of Light the Daydawn from on high,
  His dewy freshness ever strong and nigh.
Show me deliv'rance wrought by Him complete;
  Truth says without Him, "Nothing is replete."

Teach me the Name He said He had declared,
  Teach me of home, the place He has prepared.
Make clear the Door, Himself my entrance in,
  Show me the keys, the trophy He did win.

Teach me but Christ, the nations' one Desire,
  Bright hope of peace, none other can inspire.
Tell me again the Daystar shall appear,
  The Lord will come, to banish death and fear.

I am Alpha and Omega (Rev. 22:13)

Who is qualified to write a preface to One who stands in priority to all truth, who is both source and substance of all truth? How can anyone write a history of the Creator, who preceded the calendars of time and who holds precedence over all men whom He created? Journey back as far as you will, before the unnavigated ether had been stirred by angelic wing, or electro-magnetic waves were utilized (Job 38:35). Behold! He is there. Christ is the Author of the celestial fountains of mercy and of the prevalent springs of grace, which have flowed through the centuries for the welfare of mankind. Our blessed Lord is the Originator of the inscrutable purposes of righteousness and justice and the Counsellor of the immortal principles of Godhead recorded in the Scriptures. He is also the Alpha and Omega of all divine revelation. His essential energies flow and flourish in unabating fullness and felicity, for He has the dew of His youth (Ps. 110:3). As the Alpha of the alphabet He is the initial expression of infinite perfection. He is the foremost link in the chain of history and the first criterion in the volume of prophecy (Rev. 19:10).

The alphabet is a unique group of signs which signify unending utility, and in its varied forms it is used universally. Likewise also our Lord Jesus Christ is not a national or parochial Saviour over whom some select society or particular party holds exclusive claim. He is available to all. Christ is for everyone, everywhere; there is no limit to His saving power and no orbit to His proffered grace. Of this great fact His own words are very expressive, "For God so loved the world, that He gave His only begotten Son, that whosoever believeth in Him should not perish" (John 3:16). A similar far-reaching range of inclusion is rehearsed by Isaiah the prophet, "Look unto Me, and be ye saved, all the ends of the earth" (Isa. 45:22), and again, "The glory of the LORD shall be revealed, and all flesh shall see it together" (Isa. 40:5). In His sovereignty and superiority, our God is no respecter of persons, no more than sun and star to which He is likened have respect for human ancestry or posterity, nobility or dignity, poverty or royalty.

The alphabet which is so concise, comprehensive and complete is a resource for compiling words and phrases to impart knowledge, to convey comfort for the sorrowing, cheer for the serving and songs for the victorious. Hereby every form of converse, communion, condolence and communication is cared for. Again in this manifold ministry also, the alphabet unequivocally typifies Christ, in whom dwelleth all the fullness of Godhead bodily ("and ye are filled up in Him"). Yea, the complete faculties for enabling faithfulness to be expressed in witness, worship, and work, and the complete fountain of supply and sufficiency to furnish strength, sympathy and stability are resident in Him. Little wonder that Christ claimed to be the whole alphabet and all that arises from it as a medium of revelation, a reservoir of literary resource and a repository of riches in wisdom and knowledge.

Our powers of mind are as yet only in their infancy. We know in part, but in the world to come our faculties are to be adjusted to new dimensions and values. "We shall know even also as we are known," and "We shall see his face" (I Cor. 13:12; Rev. 22:4). Of all experiences this one is most to be desired, that is, a sight of the blessed Saviour. One glimpse of His glorious face and all other loveliness lessens, all other beauty blushes and all other perfection pales. The blazing splendor of infinite glory and the brilliant grandeur of immortal majesty radiate from His countenance, the light of which exceeds the sunshine in its strength. The vital fountains of friendship and the very springs of sympathy well up in His great heart of love; for He enshrines in His blessed person the solace of heaven, the sweetness of home and the sanctity of holiness. The realms where He rules reflect the riches of His replete righteousness.

In turning our attention to a group of our Lord's offices and vocations beginning with the letter "D," we shall commence with a title which represents the ever-fresh and fascinating features of sunrise.

THE DAYSPRING FROM ON HIGH

> Through the tender mercy of our God; whereby the dayspring from on high hath visited us. To give light to them that sit in darkness and in the shadow of death, to guide our feet in the way of peace (Luke 1:78).

King David had the experience of a delightful expectation when longing eagerly for a dawn that he knew would end the distractions of a distressing night that he was encountering (Ps. 130:6). The period of Palestinian history under the jurisdiction of Herod the Great, at the time these words were written, was likewise an extremely alarming record. Among other tragedies the days were darkened with a series of brutal murders. The previous high priest had been one of the victims of Herod's hateful animosity. The king's own beautiful wife together with her family had been ruthlessly slain because of suspicion. Herod's attempt to frustrate the manifestation and ministry of Messiah proved abortive, although later on he had the male children of Bethlehem destroyed, those two years old or under. On account of such conditions, when Zechariah, the officiating high priest, realized that the hour had arrived for the appearing of the long promised Messiah, and that His momentous birth had actually taken place, he broke forth in these remarkable words, "The dayspring from on high hath visited us." Christ is the One who brought into this world the magnificence of radiant goodness and revealing grace as the gifts of God's generous heart. No one could possibly have been more cordial and genial than this Visitor from above, whose appearing is likened to the smiling sunrise of a golden daybreak.

The light of this memorable dawn does not come to us via the lanes of learning or through the laborious labors of research, but by means of a Visitor from heaven, the healing rays of whose kindly light shine through the gloom of earth's moral darkness. How readily and gratefully we should welcome and worship so rare and virtuous a Visitant who comes to re-hearten, reassure and redeem the sons of men from distress and despair.

To this present hour our Lord still carries on His deliverances, not arbitrarily but as an Advocate. The effulgence of His creative splendor is not a crushing energy, but a saving evangel (II Cor. 4:6). He comes as the Balm of Gilead to the brokenhearted and binds up their wounds (Ps. 147:3), and as bright sunshine to the benighted (Mal. 4:2). The Greek words "tender mercy of our God" might be rendered "the mercy of the heart of God," which means mercy from the seat and soul of His essence. He, the All-glorious, deigns to visit us as a dawning light of lovingkindness (Isa. 9:2). Surely this is one of the finest favors of His everlasting faithfulness, which is so infinitely great and intimately gracious.

We were wholly devoid of merit or desert and without claim on His compassion; even so, from His superior station in the loftiest heavens, He condescended to shine forth and bring to us the light of the knowledge of the glory of God. A miniature suggestion of this is reflected in David at Adullum. The narrative tells us that all who were in debt, discontent or distress repaired to his cave dwelling. On arrival they looked unto him and their faces were lightened, or became radiant (Ps. 34:5).

> I was transformed
>   Into a champion of my race made strong;
> With a new courage glorying to meet
>   In all the ecstasy of sacrifice,
> Death face to face.
>
>   L. MORRIS

When we contemplate Christ as the Dayspring serving those who were stricken by suffering and stunned with sorrow we marvel at His meekness. How tender the soft radiance of His gracious tolerance, how friendly His glorious forbearance and how merciful His wondrous magnificence, all of which He harnessed to help humanity. One of the suitable prayers that fits all lips is recorded in Psalm 106:4, "O visit me." The Visitant we are considering brought to earth the spiritual light of a new daydawn with its tender mercy. In His ministry we detect the charming fragrance of the Lily of the Valleys, we discern the moral excellence of the Beauty of Holiness, we discover the ceaseless effluence of the Fountain of Life, we distinguish the comely countenance of the Beloved of the Father, we decipher the infinite patience of the Rock of Ages and detect the heart essence of the Friend of Sinners. Oh, to receive more of the sunbeams of sympathy from the Saviour's lustrous face! Some people think that Christianity consists of a dim light flickering on a drab sarcophagus in a dingy sepulcher; instead it really is the radiant glow of a resplendent Dayspring from on high.

THE DAYSMAN BETWIXT US

For He is not a man, as I am, that I should answer Him, and we should come together in judgment. Neither is there any daysman betwixt us, that might lay his hand upon us both (Job 9:32-33).

The great disadvantage man has in relation to God is the wide disparity that exists between his own nature and the character of Deity. The great Plaintiff holds a serious indictment against mankind. Damage has been done which dishonors the divine throne, and no excuse that man may make can erase the guilt or evade the penalty. The decree of heavenly justice is absolute and cannot be revoked; sin must be punished. If the Almighty were to excuse the wrong, unsullied holiness would be violated, immaculate righteousness outraged, the perfections of truth damaged, and the purity and glory of God's eternal throne imperiled. The immutable principles of God's justice are the shield and stay of heaven's age-abiding society. Injury to these would mean incalculable calamity, including the overthrow of celestial authority and the overturning of all beneficent administration. Wherefore, God in His wisdom proposes arbitration, with a view to reconciliation, in preference to the arraignment of the case in the judicial court.

In order to sponsor this intricate plan the Daysman appears and offers to meet all the claims of divine justice against sin, by the supreme sacrifice of His own perfect life. The arbitration is accepted, the Mediator suffers the death penalty and dies the just for the unjust to bring us to God, He being the only One who knows where God dwells and what God demands. The writ is now settled forever, the immutable principles of justice are upheld and fully honored, God has been glorified and sinners granted full pardon. More wonderful still, the Daysman initiates the repentant into sonship, makes each one a partaker of the divine nature and sanctifies forever more. Justice now stands with her gleaming sword triumphant while mercy is regnant in sublimest splendor (Ps. 85:10).

To qualify as Daysman it was required of Christ that He be of suitable character to associate with God and yet act for man; that He be sensible of the conditions that required settlement, and that He be serviceable in the case of both parties concerned. He has honorably discharged all obligations and has magnified the law, dignified truth, beautified grace, satisfied justice and glorified God.

My chains are snapped, the bonds of sin are broken, and I am free,
O let the triumphs of His grace be spoken, who died for me.

In undertaking this office, Christ achieved a purpose which no one else had the right or competence to fulfill. In view of his darkened conscience, man required enlightenment; and there is but one Revealer of God. In the light of man's sin-dominated life, a Ransomer from death and the grave was necessary; and Christ is the only Redeemer. On account of man's disability and distance in alienation, he stood in need of reconciliation; and Christ alone can reconcile to God. Because of man's degenerate nature, he needed to be remade; and Christ is the sole Regenerator. Our blessed Daysman secured access for the benighted, acceptance for the outcast, adoption for the stranger and association for the alien. The banished are no longer expelled but are brought back to honor, holiness, heaven and home (II Sam. 14:14; John 14:1-3).

The perfect qualifications Christ exercises prove that He wholly merits this office. His very zeal for the honor of God,

His desire for the welfare of man and His determined resolve to fulfill the purpose of heaven that the reign of righteousness might be established are among the outstanding features of His work as the Daysman. Many years ago, General Booth, the founder of the Salvation Army, led one of India's outstanding lawyers to Christ. Some time afterward that same lawyer wrote the following lines:

> He signed the deed with His redeeming blood
> And ever lives to make the payment good.
> Should sin or law or hell come in to urge a second claim,
> They all retire at once, by mention of His Name.

THE DESIRE OF ALL NATIONS

> I will shake all nations, and the desire of all nations shall come: and I will fill this house with glory, saith the Lord of hosts (Hag. 2:7).

The message of the Prophet Haggai marks the era of reconstruction in relation to the city of Jerusalem and the temple. The previous temple built by Solomon, which had stood on Mount Moriah for four hundred and ninety years, had a full complement of significant symbols and suggestive types which represented higher spiritual realities. These shadows of better things to come were given to attract attention and draw out the real devotion of the nation of Israel in worship. Types and symbols, however, never maintain loyalty of aspiration and adoration for long. On this account, when the returned exiles from the captivity in Babylon had reconstructed the city and temple, the rebuilt edifice was denied the five most desirable symbols—those of the ark of the covenant with its mercy seat, the tables of the law, the holy fire, the sacred oracle and the Shekinah glory. These had been but tentative shadows of the true substance, which is Christ. He is in reality the expression of the glory of God, He is the genuine Oracle through whom God speaks; He is the Mercy Seat for our sins and is pledged in this prophecy to come to the rebuilt temple, that the glory of this latter house may be greater than the former.

The blessed One came and the Apostle John records, "We beheld His glory, the glory as of the only begotten of the Father, full of grace and truth." Christ Himself said, "In this place is one greater than the temple" (Matt. 12:6). Wherefore in the context He gave the invitation, "Come unto Me, all ye that labor and are heavy laden, and I will give you rest" (Matt. 11:28). The Desire of all nations, the divine Mediator, had come and announced the assurance, "Him that cometh to Me I will in no wise cast out" (John 6:37). "No man cometh unto the Father, but by Me" (John 14:6). Therefore He is the Desire of all those who wish to come to the eternal Father, to His holy habitation and heavenly heritage.

The greatest desire the world over is to find one who is able to lead us back to God, to love, to light, to life, to liberty and to everlastingness. The brightest promise of God's blessed favor is the guarantee that He would send such an One. Who but the Spirit of God could foresee this to foretell it? Who could have given the types without knowing what they were to typify?

How dearly we should cherish such a treasure as we have in Christ. He is like the rich spices that breathe out their own perfume. His very vesture is tinged with the vermilion of splendor and the azure of hope. His virtues are holy in honor and His victories are flaming with fame. How we should magnify and glorify this precious One who is so admirably suited in affinity and able to meet the greatest need of mankind. When we pause to consider His matchless name of priceless merit, of changeless might, of ceaseless music and of endless song, we know well that without Him there would be no truth of saving grace, no touch of spiritual healing, no title of abiding sonship, no trumpet of jubilee, no triumph over death, no thornless paradise, no tearless society and no tombless world to come. What an heirloom! The marvel of it! The wonder of it! How amazing is the goodness of God! The Desire of all nations, the merciful Mediator, Reconciler and Redeemer, came.

"Art thou He that should come, or look we for another?" asked the mighty prophet, John. Nay, none other can ever be like Him. He of all celebrities is most to be desired, the choicest, loveliest, fairest, chiefest, the altogether lovely and lovable, both in His kingship as King of kings and His lordship as Lord of lords. As the one Mediator between God and men, Christ is of all most desirable, without rival in His regal beauty, without equal in His royal majesty, without parallel in His faithful constancy, and without sequel in His eternal finality.

THE DELIVERER OF ZION

> And it shall come to pass, that whosoever shall call on the name of the LORD shall be delivered: for in Mount Zion and in Jerusalem shall be deliverance, as the LORD hath said (Joel 2:32; also II Sam. 22:2; Ps. 144:2).

The Apostles Peter and Paul resort to this prophecy of Joel when they desire to describe the deliverance which is wrought in lives through preaching the Evangel (Acts 2:21; Rom. 10:13). The power and purpose of this Deliverer remain unchanged and undiminished. The everlasting doom from which He is able to deliver is also just as real. The Word of God does not contain antiquated notions about which men of advanced views are free to make jests. Christ, with His unclouded vision of the future, warned of coming judgment with tear-filled eyes. He offered to His hearers complete deliverance (John 5:24).

The immortal brow of this divine Deliverer glitters with imperial diadems of conquest (Rev. 19:12). He possesses coronets of compassion that outshine all the comely crowns of earthly majesty. He wears wreaths of worthiness that never wilt or wither. He possesses garlands of grace that glisten with glory unspeakable. Christ holds a sovereign scepter of saving strength which He sways for the deliverance of all who are depressed, defiled, or defeated; for "Whosoever shall call on the name of the Lord shall be delivered" (Joel 2:32). No ditch bars the way to His wonderful help; it matters not whether the suppliant is disgruntled or debased; provisos and peradventures are nonexistent. "Whosoever calls" is the only qualification for deliverance.

He plucks the defenseless prey from the merciless jaws of the cruel monster and in so doing delivers the captives (Luke 4:18). The Apostle Paul states, "Who delivered us from so great a death" (II Cor. 1:10). We were hemmed in between defiles narrower than the Gorge of Gondo in the higher Alps and were more closely confined than the troops under General Napier between the precipitous cliffs of the Seneffe Pass in northern Ethiopia. Christ traversed the treacherous vale of threatening gloom alone, overcame the foe and opened a highway that leads more and more to the perfect day. He overpowered oppression in order to bestow full liberty to the children of God and He overthrew the obstacles that denied us advance so as to lead us step by step in the path of triumph (II Cor. 2:14).

We may venture our all on this Victor because He has already vanquished the enemy and always wins the victory. David could say, "My soul trusteth in Thee: yea, in the shadow of Thy wings will I make my refuge, until these calamities be overpast" (Ps. 57:1). Joel tells of a dread day when the sun shall be darkened and the moon crimsoned so that in that hour of tragic calamity we shall be glad indeed that we have a Deliverer. Reverence and reliance following on repentance are befitting attitudes on our part toward this great and gracious Emancipator, whom the weakest may worship and the poorest praise.

No one but Christ has a fame that spans the centuries as a Deliverer, nor a name that soars highest as a Defender, nor a claim that stands foremost as a Distributer of spiritual blessings to furnish the insignificant sons of men with innumerable privileges and inestimable advantages which are age-abiding. To the free He becomes a veritable constellation of favors, a mansion of mercies, a citadel of comforts, a residence of riches and a dwelling of delights. What a Deliverer!

THE DEW OF ISRAEL

I will be as the dew unto Israel: he shall grow as the lily
and cast forth his roots as Lebanon. His branches shall
spread, and his beauty shall be as the olive tree (Hos.
14:5).

Christ makes His people what He is Himself. He has the dew
of His youth and this amaranthine freshness of vigor, virtue
and vision He imparts to His redeemed to make them partakers of His divine nature. Who is not familiar with the
fascinating features of early morning freshness sparkling with
dewdrops which scintillate like costly jewels in the clear
sunlight, adding a rare beauty to the foliage, flowers and fruits
of the late springtide and early summer? If these delicate
transparent touches of beauty which the dewdrops add to the
delights of the garden are so lovely, what are we to say of the
lasting luster of Christ's loveliness, characteristics which He
has pledged to reveal to those that love Him (I Cor. 2:9). If the
transient dew is so fair and fascinating in its attractive charm,
what will the higher spiritual reality be like, when the soul is
enriched and engraced with the spiritual virtues and vitalities
which are ever fresh and fragrant?

We should remember that this beautiful luster of pearl-like
splendor which is signified in the dew is a permanent feature
in our beloved Christ. Of Him it is written, "In the beauties of
holiness from the womb of the morning: Thou hast the dew of
Thy youth" (Ps. 110:3). So the passing figure of the transient is
lifted from its temporal setting and made to become a symbol
of the permanent feature of freshness and fairness in Christ's
character and is used to express His perpetual vigor of unchanging youthfulness. We know assuredly that His vitality
never varies, His fervor never flags, His agility never ages, His
fortitude never fails, His feet never falter, His will never
wavers, His dominion never declines, His constancy never
changes, His beauty never blemishes and His face never
furrows; for He has the dew of His youth eternally. He is the
ageless, timeless Lover who pledges to be the same to His

people in freshness and fullness forever. What felicity and fruitfulness this fact should assure to every believing heart!

We have proved definitely that fine clothes cannot content the heart of man; he needs the garment of glory and robe of righteousness to gratify his desire. Fragrant flowers cannot satiate the soul, but the everlasting Rose of Sharon and ever-living Lily of the Valleys can fulfill this requirement. Costly couches cannot console the broken spirit, but the comfort of God can do it. Nor can scientific research fill the quest of the mind. We need a replete Christ to achieve it, "in whom are hid all the treasures of wisdom and knowledge." Not by walking a golden street, not by playing a golden harp, not by wearing a golden crown can the soul of man find rest, but only in the glorious Christ, the gracious Son of man, the gorgeous Lord of lords and King of kings, who is all the fullness of Godhead bodily.

Men are continually searching the rocks for minerals, scouring the oyster beds for pearls, scanning the mines for jewels and scrutinizing the strata for geological secrets. Try to imagine if you will, an object of eternal interest, a study that survives the ages, a subject that supersedes all others, because the character of the One contemplated is infinite. We may incessantly investigate Christ and concentrate all our attention upon Him, because He is inexhaustible. This is true of the beauty of His holiness, the bounty of His goodness, the beams of His righteousness, the bloom of His preciousness and the gleams of His loveliness, all of which are centered in the one Bridegroom of abiding freshness, who shines forth with the dew of His youth. We may bring all the examining powers of skill and wisdom to bear upon Him, only to find yet more amazing expressions and exhibitions of His eternal ex-cellences, which speak to the soul with unrivalled eloquence.

Christ is the fullness of the highest glories, deepest mysteries and sweetest secrets of everlasting light, life, and love. New specialties will be ceaselessly unveiled from the boundless fields of His knowledge and the shoreless seas of His wisdom, which are likewise ever fresh and fruitful. In His dew-drenched vigorous life He will be as the dew to the whole Israel of God

(Gal. 6:16), that numberless host which will reflect His image, resemble His likeness and revel in His lovingkindness forever. Think of it!

Today man is able to turn the telescope from planet to planet, star to star, cluster to cluster, constellation to constellation and discover new wonders in the heavens continuously in what seemingly appears to be a limitless universe. But to whom are we to liken the Creator of all this, who bears no marks of age and wears no wrinkles of weariness in His perfect countenance? With thousands of years of human history behind us, we yet face unnavigated seas of ether, uninvestigated stretches of stellar space and unexplored sections of ponderous constellations. Yet, withal, these material things are nothing to be compared with the towering magnificence of the changeless Christ, who is to be the subject of study and object of worship eternally. What an occupation lies ahead of us—examining His excellences, peering into His perfections, viewing His virtues, considering His comelinesses, searching His splendors, recounting His resources, admiring His abilities, beholding His beauties, adoring His attributes and gazing upon His glories endlessly. What will it mean?

We shall then possess perfected capacities capable of indefinite development with an ever maturing appreciation of the Saviour's sublimities. He is the Treasure without a terminus, the Blesser without a boundary and the Light without a limit. The locks of His hair are bushy and black and never perish, the glint of His eyes is keen and kindly and never dims, the spirit of His mind is bright and buoyant and never dulls, the pulse of His affection is strong and steady and never weakens, the power of His hand is mighty and majestic and never tires.

Never can there be any lack of balance in His perfect character to blur His beauty, or lack of sincerity to stain His sanctity, or lack of joy to jar His jubilation, or lack of memory to mar His mindfulness, nor any lack of harmony to harm His holiness. He abides the same enduringly. O Christ, let Thy beauty be upon us and establish Thou the work of our hands (Ps. 90:17).

Let the beauty of Jesus be seen in me,
   All His wonderful passion and purity;
   Oh, Thou Spirit divine, all my nature refine
   Till the beauty of Jesus is seen in me.

THE DISCERNER OF THE HEART

> For the word of God is quick, and powerful, and sharper than any twoedged sword, piercing even to the dividing asunder of soul and spirit, and of joints and marrow, and is a discerner of the thoughts and intents of the heart. Neither is there any creature that is not manifest in His sight (Heb. 4:12).

Here is an instance where the inspired God-breathed Word, and the incarnate God-manifested Word are inseparably linked. Christ is incarnate in the revelation of truth as well as in the manifestation of truth. The Word embodies Christ, Christ embodies the Word. In the book of Revelation, with its significant symbols, these two are again definitely identified, both coincide (Rev. 3:12). They both warm hearts and warn hearers, furnish comfort and flash censure, both can surely save or severely smite. So let us also weave the two into one, for that which God hath joined let no man put asunder. The Saviour and the Scriptures each exert a quickening, soul-saving power, an indescribable vitality which breathes either censure or comfort, and blesses in conditions of scarcity or sufficiency, want or wealth. We cannot therefore presume to accept the Christ of God if we reject the Word of God, for these agree in one. If we accept the Revealer we must accept His Revelation. If we pay homage to the Son, let us also honor the Scriptures. We dare not deride His Word if we decide to accept His will.

The actual Greek word used here is *kritikos* from which we derive our word "critic," and the passage as a whole, which covers verses 12 and 13, declares that Christ has a deciding power because He is living and powerful; a discriminating power, differentiating between soul and spirit; a dissecting power, detecting the thoughts and intents of the heart; and a discovering power, disclosing all things openly concerning everyone, everywhere. He is able to detect between the natural demand and the spiritual desire, sentimental decision and sacrificial dedication, self-advancement and self-abandonment. We may evade detection by man with our dodging and twisting; we cannot elude Him who knows our innermost thoughts and intentions.

We are definitely assured that effective power, efficient protection and effectual purpose are alike dispensed by the Word of the Lord and by the Lord of the Word. The context of this portion links His priestly work with His precious Word. The sure Word of the Scriptures safeguards the soul from danger, while the steadfast Priest supplicates for deliverance. Combined, these two Sentinels of Mercy guard and guide our feet in ways of righteousness. All too frequently the comforts we enjoy in life mar our useful service more than the conflicts we encounter. Chiefly because we are assailable in so many vulnerable points, God reminds us of the indispensable resources He has made available to meet all circumstances. His promise and His presence are assured to every worshipper, warrior, worker and witness at all times. Every trial should be turned to a triumph that we might have a more glowing testimony to give for Him.

THE DEFENDER AND REFUGE

But the Lord is my defence; and my God is the rock of my refuge (Ps. 94:22; also 59:9; Isa. 37:35).

At every stage in life we need defense, even from our youngest years to oldest age. This is occasioned by our living in the midst of destructive forces wielded by the destroyer, the dread Apollyon, which is always on the alert. Youthful minds also need guarding against the detrimental, deceitful and defiling influences of life. The chief centers and cities of our civilization likewise need defense. When Jerusalem was jeopardized by the blasphemous threat of Rab-shakeh of Assyria, King Hezekiah asked the Prophet Isaiah to take the ultimatum and lay it before the living God. The prophet received the heartening reply, "I will defend this city to save it for Mine own sake, and for My servant David's sake" (Isa. 37:35), and the message was conveyed to the king (II Kings 19:34). When Alexander the Great was marching up the coast of Palestine with his forty thousand braves, the Lord pledged to defend the newly built temple and the people at Jerusalem (Zech. 9:8,13,15).

These historical records, which show the displays of divine power in the visible world, form a picturesque background to reflect the greater defense provided against diabolical foes. We cannot of ourselves assail the strongholds of the Devil. We are impotent to turn the tides of the Tempter's treachery or the torments of Tantalus. We cannot counter the forces of the foe and conquer death or cancel sin, but Christ can and He is our Defender. His defense is not only for civil, communal and national life, He also guards our personal, moral and spiritual interests.

When David was surrounded by wicked men he declared confidently, "God is my defence" (Ps. 59:9,16,17), and was able to record that the degree of joy he experienced through trust was "Because thou defendest" (Ps. 5:11). In our title Psalm it is written, "The Lord is my defence; and my God is the rock of my refuge" (Ps. 94:22). He, as my Defender, is never careless or careworn, never wearied or worried, never indifferent or impotent, and is never disinterested or distracted; so why should I be disquieted or disturbed? When friends fail and foes frustrate, when prospects pale and possessions perish, why fidget and fret, why not rely and rest? For He is most desirable and dependable as a Defender. "Thou hast a mighty arm: strong is Thy hand, and high is Thy hand" (Ps. 89:13). We should gladly break forth into singing, "Sufficient is Thine arm alone, and our defence is sure."

Christ in person is our Defender. He it was that stood beside the three heroes and defended them from the flaming furnace; He defended Daniel from the brute beasts of the den wherein he was cast; He defended Paul before Agrippa and Nero and delivered him out of the mouth of the lion; He defended Peter in the dungeon and also delivered him. He is likewise "our Shield and Defender, the Ancient of Days, pavilioned in splendor, and girded with praise." Christ readily responds to danger signals whenever they are visible, as in the temple court He defended an accused woman, removed her condemnation and empowered her to withstand temptation. Lord, "cover my defenseless head with the shadow of Thy wing." Christ is an almighty Defender and is always attentive and active on behalf of His people. He provides the canopy to shelter us, the panoply to shield us (Eph. 6:11) and the majesty to support us; yea, underneath are the everlasting arms. He is well able to defend us from every danger and deliver even from darkness and death.

> Thou, O Christ, art all I want;
>   More than all in Thee I find;
> Raise the fallen, cheer the faint,
>   Heal the sick and lead the blind.

> Just and holy is Thy Name,
>   I am all unrighteousness;
> False and full of sin I am,
>   Thou art full of truth and grace.

THE DECLARER OF THE NAME

I have declared unto them Thy name, and will declare it: that the love wherewith Thou hast loved Me may be in them, and I in them (John 17:26).

As a mighty Alpine peak overtops the minor hills and casts its restful shadow along the vale below, so one of the loftiest aims in Christ's ministry during His manifestation was to declare the Father, and this witness looms largest across the whole landscape of John's message. The revelation of the Father brought to us by Christ is the supreme summit of Christianity. Out of one hundred and thirty nine references to the name "Father" in John's Gospel, all but sixteen refer to the Father of glory. No one knows the Father but the Son; therefore no one else is qualified for such a ministry. The Son has finally revealed the Father and nothing can be added to what Christ disclosed. Christ has also faithfully represented the Father and fully resembled Him in all His ways.

We only need to reflect on the Son's ministry and view Him hushing the winds, calming the waves, stilling the storms, expelling the demons, healing the sick, feeding the multitudes, cleansing the lepers, forgiving the sins, raising the dead, quenching the thirst, imparting the life, delivering the captives, and scores of other activities in all of which he declares the Father. The Son knows the Father's will and came to fulfill it; the Son beholds the Father's worthiness and came to bear witness to Him; the Son receives the Father's words and came to speak them (John 8:28-29).

At the very beginning of His ministry Christ declared the ineffable glory of the Father (John 1:14). He testified to the inestimable ability of the Father's power (5:21). He affirmed the infinite integrity of the Father's faithful care (14:23). He stressed the intrinsic beauty of the Father's boundless love (16:27). He described the immortal identity of the Father's shepherd sympathy (10:27-30). He explained the inimitable society of the Father's spacious house (14:2). These are but a few of the many features of the Father's infinite transcendence which Christ advocated. He gave us to understand clearly that the Father's exquisite excellence exceeds all human knowledge, that His superior sufficiency surmounts all earthly calculation and that His superlative sympathy supersedes the totality of finite capacity to comprehend. As Son of God, Christ claimed to have altogether expressed the true and vital characteristics of the Father by demonstrating scores of the choicest exhibitions of His care. He showed that meekness was not weakness, but majestic might harnessed to minister to mankind. The Son with His sincere heart of humility was the living exegete of God, bearing every mark of majesty, sharing every merit of ministry, evincing every feature of fidelity, showing every service of sympathy, yea, and exercising every desirable faculty for the saving and satisfying of men. "Shew us the Father and it contenteth us," said Philip; the very thing which Christ had already done.

In looking back over His work, how memorable His eloquence (John 7:46); how remarkable His reticence (8:6); how desirable His diligence (9:4); how creditable His conscience (8:7, 46); how peaceable His patience and how seasonable His radiance. No extremes or excesses marred His representation; no faults or failures scarred His resemblance; no single feature of His character was disproportionate or deficient. His life was a vessel of blended beauty and charming courtesy, perfectly balanced in every detail. Every essential element of excellence embodied in the Father was worthily enshrined in the Son; therefore He could say unreservedly, "He that hath seen Me hath seen the Father" (14:9), and again, "I have glorified Thee on earth; I have finished the work which Thou gavest Me to do" (17:4). Right at the close of His work He referred to having glorified the Father by virtue of four facilities given to Him, and He imparts these same four to His disciples to enable them to glorify Him: the Word, the Commission, the Glory and the Love are the same as Christ received (17:8,18,22,23).

The Gospel of John is a wonderful unveiling of the perfect harmony of the Father and the Son, which verifies Christ's profound claim, "I and My Father are one" (10:30). Let us tabulate a score of these features in demonstration of oneness.

> Purpose to Purpose — 3:16,17;12:27
> Work to Work — 5:17,19; 9:4
> Life to Life — 5:26
> Gift to Gift — 4:10
> Doctrine to Doctrine — 7:16
> Word to Word — 8:47; 15:9; 17:24
> Mind to Mind — 10:15
> Hand to Hand — 10:28,29
> Face to Face — 11:41; 17:1
> Will to Will — 5:30; 6:38
> Honor to Honor — 5:23
> Authority to Authority — 5:27
> Witness to Witness — 5:36; 8:18
> Company to Company — 8:29
> Power to Power — 10:18
> Love to Love — 10:17; 15:9; 17:24

Likeness to Likeness—14:9
Claim to Claim—16:15; 17:10
Heart to Heart—17:21, 22
Glory to Glory—12:28; 13:31; 32; 17:5

THE DOOR OF THE SHEEP

Verily, verily, I say unto you, I am the door of the
sheep (John 10:7).

Many famous doors exist in this world which give access to
the privileges and advantages of various societies and their
fellowships; but foremost of all in both value and veneration is
the one here named. This declaration which Christ made in
the precincts of the temple in Solomon's porch (v. 23) is
directly descriptive of Himself as being the way of entrance
and means of access to eternal life and full salvation. Christ
introduced Himself as the Door that we might have an introduction to the innermost of immortality (v. 9). Yea, He is
the Door of invitation to initiate His people into the illustrious
society of the saved (v.9). He is also the Door of interrelation
between God and man, heaven and earth, life and death, that
we may become intimately identified with the fellowship of the
family circle of the Father's house (14:2). Christ is the only one
who can give to man the right of access to the Father (14:6).
He declared to His disciples at the beginning of His ministry
that they were to see heaven opened (1:51), which means
nothing less than a revealed way for man's return to God by
reconciliation, first visualized in Jacob's vision and
materialized in the Saviour's mediation. Other than Christ no
one else can open heaven to man.

When we enter this Door we experience a liberation from
the burden of anxiety, the bondage of agony and the bane of
adversity. Encounters of this kind can no longer endanger our
liberty. Then again on the other side of the picture, we, the
participants of the elect society, are made to partake of
essential satiety and are perfected in eternal security (10:28).

> The Cross of Christ is verily our plea,
> Himself the Door to immortality for you and me,
> And He is near us for our access free,
> To dwell in light and love and purity.

While I visited the city of Milan in northern Italy, my attention was directed to the three imposing doors at the front of the great cathedral. Over each of the doors there is an inscription chiseled in the stone. Above the right hand portal is sculptured a wreath of flowers, and beneath it are the words, "All that pleases is but for a moment." Over the entrance on the left is a sculptured cross and at the top end a crown of thorns, bearing the motto, "All that troubles is but for a moment." Over the central door there is simply a sentence without a symbol, which reads, "Nothing is important save that which is eternal." The things seen are temporal (II Cor. 4:18); and if we would enter into the realities of the eternal, Christ is the only door of admittance.

THE DIVIDER OF DAY AND NIGHT

> And God said, Let there be light: and there was light.
> And God saw the light that it was good: and God divided
> the light from the darkness (Gen. 1:3-4; see also Deut.
> 5:28; Neh. 9:11; Dan. 5:28; Matt. 25:32; Luke 12:13-
> 14).

The Creator of all things has been the great Divider from the beginning. On the opening page of Genesis He divided light from darkness, day from night, and land from water, all of which divisions are outside the range of human ability. He also divided the nations (Gen. 10:5), and in Peleg's day He divided the earth (Gen. 10:25). During the national history of Israel He gave a law which divided between good and evil, right and wrong, truth and error, clean and unclean, holy and unholy, and all other features that were in keeping with the moral standards of righeousness. When our Lord was manifested He introduced the great divide into our almanacs and calendars of time. During His ministry He taught the same directing principle in His parables concerning the wheat and tares of the field, the good and bad in the dragnet, and the sheep and goats among nations.

Christ divides in order that He may gather the good, He differentiates that He may garner the wheat and he discriminates that He may greet His sheep with those special words of welcome, "Come, ye blessed of My Father, inherit the kingdom prepared for you from the foundation of the world" (Matt. 25:34). He came to divide between degenerate and regenerate, that he might "gather together in one the children of God that were scattered abroad" (John 11:52; see also Eph. 1:9-10)

A man's policy, philosophy and philanthropy may appear to be commendable but if they be out of harmony with Christ, such an one is opposed to Him. If the fruit and fragrance of your life are not factors in influencing others to follow Christ the finest claim you may make of serving in His interests is false; but if you crown and coronate Him Lord, then others are sure to follow as the result of your witness.

THE DAYSTAR TO ARISE

> We have also a more sure word of prophecy; whereunto
> ye do well that ye take heed, as unto a light that shineth
> in a dark place, until the day dawn, and the daystar arise
> in your hearts (II Pet. 1:19).

The lofty lineage of the Light-bringer is suggested by the use of the star. Christ is matchless in underived majesty and fadeless in unconferred glory. The daystar is the officially ordained sign of oncoming dawn. Peter uses it as the omen of omnipotence which directs our hearts to the Overcomer of all darkness and the Originator of all light. This special designation clearly stipulates the supernatural distinction and superior dominion of the Christ, who must needs return and reign in righteousness, after establishing His everlasting kingdom in a new earth (Isa. 66:22).

The reality of all this the sceptic disdains with open scorn. The heretic distorts the same by disregarding the balance of truth. The cynic despises it as something utterly ridiculous. The fanatic defames it by unwarrantable excesses in interpretation. The pedant decries it because it is outside the orbit of his comprehension. The mimic disputes it and reverts to past historical happenings as an apparent fulfillment, while the neurotic denounces it as mere sensationalism. However, despite these derogatory attitudes, the Christian cherishes it as being the brightest ray in the eastern sky of hope.

Let us remember that the perfect luster of light, the princely scepter of lordship and the precious miter of love are centered within the jurisdiction of this Daystar, while the dazzling brightness of His dignified brilliance betokens the suitability of His steadfast character for universal control. The hour of His arising and appearing will herald the final victory over darkness, and also honor the faithful Victor who overcame the Devil and death. Darkness will never again regain her woeful empire and the Devil will not again resume his wicked enterprise. Let us bow our heads in reverent worship as we contemplate the luminosity of light, the brilliance of beauty and the permanency of power which characterize our Daystar. As chiefest among celestial celebrities, He will one day shine forth in the sublimity of His undefined splendor to usher in eternal day. "Who in the heaven can be compared unto the LORD? who among the sons of the mighty can be likened unto the LORD?" (Ps. 89:6, 7)

How entirely independent of all earthly imperialism and dictatorship a star is; therefore it sets forth in worthy representation the majestic superiority of the great administrator. With a regularity unbroken and a consistency unshaken, this superb symbol appears in the sky morning by morning to herald the approach of each new day. As a sign, the star reflects the eternal authority and enduring constancy which are resident in Christ, combined with those other features of permanent abiding and pre-eminent adjudication which are His. We also see emblazoned in this stately figure of supremacy, the effulgent excellence of the gracious Emancipator, who sways the sovereign scepter of all power in heaven and on earth. What will it be to behold His return, when He comes to usher in that halcyon day of warless delights?

The coming of Christ as the Daystar is not simply a subject for theological discussion, nor is it merely a specialty for a class called students of prophecy; it is rather one of the essential doctrines of eschatology, one of the vital truths of the New Testament and one of the most practical teachings of Christ and His apostles. Yes, His coming in glory is a matter which has a bearing on the life and labors of every Christian. Twenty-six of the imperative commands of the Gospels and Epistles are related to this event: for example, "take heed," "be ready," "gird up your loins," "look up," "watch," "be patient," "occupy till I come," and the like. Wherefore, it behooves us to live consistently, labor ceaselessly and look constantly for Christ, as warriors who war a good warfare, and as watchers who work and worship while waiting.

THE DISSOLVER OF ALL THINGS

> Seeing then that all these things shall be dissolved, what manner of persons ought ye to be in all holy conversation and godliness, looking for and hasting unto the coming of the day of God, wherein the heavens being on fire shall be dissolved, and the elements shall melt with fervent heat? (II Pet. 3:11-12)

The Prophet Daniel was acclaimed "the dissolver of doubts" by the Queen of Babylon, but he gave the credit for this ability to his divine Lord; for of a truth Christ is certainly the One who dissolves doubts. He is also the One who solves the secrets of the seven seals by virtue of His sacrificial merit and His coronation at the right hand of the Most High (Rev. 6). Furthermore, in view of His administrative power He is yet to become the Dissolver of a degenerate world (Isa. 24:1,19).

Some folk say that God is indifferent about what goes on in the world and ignores the things which individuals and nations are doing. The Apostle Peter strongly protests against such reasoning, and affirms that the visitations of God are clearly vouched for and verified all through history. He quotes, for instance, Noah's day as did also our Lord (Luke 17:26-27), and declares that on that occasion the unprecedented instrument of devastation God used for overthrow was a tremendous flood, but that the destruction to come will be carried out by the use of fire, which will dissolve all things.

Mockers on the other hand tell us there is no evidence of the existence of God or that He exercises jurisdiction over the world, for "all things," they say, "continue as they were from the beginning of the creation" (II Pet. 3:4). Peter predicted that this fallacy of the eternity of matter would be aired by scoffers in the last days. Such a theory has already been exploded by the discovery of atomic power. More than two and a half millenniums ago, the Prophet Isaiah assured us that the earth would be clean dissolved (Isa. 24:19). Christ Himself affirmed that heaven and earth would pass away (Matt. 24:35). The Apostle Peter adds, "Seeing that all these things shall be dissolved, what manner of persons ought ye to be" (II Pet. 3:11). No fossil or fabric is formidable enough to resist the fierce flame and fervent heat of that day.

Christ the Creator knows the constituents and chemical content of every element. He has weighed the earth in a balance, which means that every element is measured and its content compacted proportionately. Oxygen can now be extracted from the hardest rock or flinty marble by applying sufficient heat, and hydrogen can be taken from water by passing through it a high voltage of electricity. These elements of oxygen and hydrogen are two of the greatest factors in combustion. When placed together in acetylene gas and ignited, they burn through the toughest steel. All that is necessary is for Christ, in whom all things cohere, to derange the balance of these two elements and the combustion of the entire earth would immediately follow. Professor James Jeans wrote in one of his later books, "The whole available evidence seems to indicate that solid matter forever melts into unsubstantial radiation; forever the tangible changes into the intangible."

We cannot interpret such things as some do, by speaking of these world events as the inevitable results of natural causes; for they constitute an intentional inaugurated purpose, instituted by divine decree (Isa. 46:9-10). The Bible is the only book in the world that supplies an accurate account of the commencement of creation, furnishes details on the course of the centuries and forecasts the consummation at the close of the age. These things are plainly portrayed in the Scriptures by the omniscient Christ, the thought of whose coming encourages earnestness, energizes endeavor and engenders expectation.

> Oh, when heaven and earth are passing,
>   Crumbling as a burning scroll,
> Is there no abiding foothold,
>   No fixed refuge for the soul?
>
> Yes, a man, the Man Christ Jesus,
>   On the wreck of time He stands
> And the souls of countless millions
>   Lie within His pierced hands.

E

This casket of credentials portrays the illimitable, inexhaustible, indispensable and indestructible glories of Christ. His ineffable character supercedes and trancends all.

The EVERLASTING TO EVERLASTING (Ps. 90:2)
> Without variableness or shadow of turning.

The EMMANUEL, GOD WITH US (Matt. 1:23)
> Revealer of God and Ratifier of promise.

The ENSIGN OF THE PEOPLE (Isa. 11:10)
> Christ is to be the global center of authority.

The EXCELLENCY OF GOD (Isa. 35:2)
> Loftiest in beauty and sublimity.

The ETERNAL GOD (Deut. 33:27)
> Unfailing in security and sympathy.

The ENGRAVER OF THE NAME (Isa. 49:16)
> Reliable in fixity and faithfulness.

The ESTIMATOR OF VALUES (Luke 5:5)
> The true compensator of all consecration.

The ESTABLISHER OF COVENANTS (Gen. 9:17)
> Integrity that is immutable.

The EXECUTOR OF JUDGMENT (John 5:27)
> Unerring in discernment and decision.

The ELECT SERVANT (Isa. 42:1-4)
> Impossible of failure in anything.

The EXPRESS IMAGE (Heb. 1:3)
> The exact prototype of God.

The END (Rev. 21:6)
> The continual One the Consummator.

THE BRIGHTNESS OF GOD'S GLORY

Christ Expressed

The friendly affinity of fatherly authority
The devout integrity of divine immutability
The generous legacy of glorious liberality
The humble courtesy of holy constancy
The manifold ministry of majestic mercy
The wealthy sympathy of worthy sublimity
The healthy sanctity of heavenly sincerity
The manifest majesty of mediative mystery

THE EXPRESS IMAGE OF HIS PERSON

Image of the Father, true to likeness He,
Semblance of Jehovah, evermore to be.
Wholly One in purpose, One in mind and will,
Son of God most truly, ever faithful still.

Friendly in Thy mercy, fervent in Thy love
Christly in Thy bounty, so like God above,
Fragrant are Thy footprints, boundless in Thy care,
Altogether glorious, worshipfully fair.

Higher than the holy, mightier than the strong,
Greater in Thy glory than the heavenly throng.
Richer than the wealthy, saintlier than the wise,
Fairer in Thy beauty, than the azure skies.

Brighter than the lofty, lovelier than the light,
Nobler than the faithful clad in raiment white.
Sweeter than the honey, is Thy precious Name,
Deeper in its myst'ry, than Shekinah's flame.

Meekest in Thy service, loftiest is Thy might
Kingliest in Thy patience, Champion for the right,
Grandest in Thy merit, foremost in Thy claim,
Jesus ever worthy, glory to Thy Name.

I am Alpha and Omega (Rev. 22:13).

Christ is before language and beyond it; therefore the witness He bore personally to the Father, to Himself and to the Spirit of truth surpasses in word formation, sentence construction and symbolic representation every other testimony in existence. The majestic style that characterizes His words of witness, and with majestic style, both vividness and vitalizing energy, are not found in the speech of any other herald: "Never man spake like this man" (John 7:46). What is more, the final declaration which Christ made to the Apostle John on Patmos concerning Himself is the most complete statement of claim He ever uttered and supplies a brighter and broader illustration of His own personal infinitude than is given elsewhere in the Scriptures. The renowned range of its message assures us that in personality, in potentiality and in prerogative, He is infinite. The alphabet, to which Christ draws special attention by advancing this title, is one of the illimitable things we make use of in this world. The inexhaustible resources, indestructible records and indispensable reasons attached to the alphabet defy all our explanations.

Firstly, the inexhaustibility of resource, which is signified by the alphabetical signs, finds an irrefutable demonstration in the learning and literature handed down through the centuries. The letters themselves can never be outworn, outclassed, or outgrown. The alphabet is everlastingly important, and never becomes impotent or decrepit with age, nor does it become incompetent because of excessive demands made upon it.

Secondly, the indestructibility of the records compiled from the letters of the alphabet is assured chiefly by the fact of revelation. Speech is the medium of communication in the celestial realms of abiding society. The song of Moses, the servant of God, sung at the time of the Red Sea deliverance, is to be sung by a host that no man can number beside the crystal sea (Rev. 15:2-3). We are also notified that the Word of God liveth and abideth forever: "Forever O Lord, Thy word is settled in heaven" (Ps. 119:89). This statement thoroughly confirms the fact that not one of the official and vocational titles of Christ can ever become obsolete and not a single name He bears can ever go into oblivion. Every letter of the alphabet is used repeatedly when enumerating His multiform titles and designations; wherefore we have the guarantee that its signs can never be destroyed. Speech survives the centuries, words abide the ages; for the eternal God speaks.

Thirdly, the indispensable reasons for the alphabet are surely apparent to all; it is inconceivable to us that anything else could serve as a substitute. In the light of these things we are confident that to a far greater degree than we have suggested, the Christ of God, who is the Alpha and Omega, is certainly indestructible; He is definitely inexhaustible and He is positively indispensable. How appropriately real and how absolutely true these three features become when applied to Him of whom the Apostle Paul wrote, "Which in His times He shall shew, who is the blessed and only Potentate, the King of kings, and Lord of lords; who only hath immortality, dwelling in light which no man can approach unto; whom no man hath seen, nor can see: to whom be honour and power everlasting. Amen" (I Tim. 6:15-16).

As the Alpha and Omega, Christ is the only way to the sacred splendor of spiritual secrets (Rev. 2:17); He is the solitary key to unlock the transcendent treasures of un-tarnished truth, Himself the Interpreter of all the intricacies and realities of the invisible (Rev. 3:7). Yea, He is the one exclusive Door of entrance to the exhaustless ecstasies of eternal enjoyment (Ps. 16:11; John 10:9). Furthermore, He is the sole "Heir of all things" (Heb. 1:2); therefore the only One with infinite merit that can impart to us the title to inherit unfading glories as joint heirs. The verities He bestows are the legacies of everlasting love. Our Saviour is not only our steadfast security, He is the one incomparable portal to admit and promote our access to the perennial springs of abounding peace and abiding satisfaction (Eph. 2:18; Ps. 17:15). At this point our meditation directs us to twelve of Christ's titles and offices beginning with the letter "E."

THE EVERLASTING TO EVERLASTING

> LORD, Thou hast been our dwelling place in all generations. Before the mountains were brought forth, or ever Thou hadst formed the earth and the world, even from everlasting to everlasting, Thou art God (Ps. 90:2).

How utterly out of keeping with the transient nature of man is this striking feature of the Maker of all things, as expressed by these words. The capacity of the human mind cannot calculate divine persons who are without commencement and devoid of consummation. We are so circumscribed and confined by the tentativeness of time and the temporal limitations of life that in our case beginnings and boundaries seem inevitable. If we stop to consider, we find that we are unable to trace the first or final league of azure sky; so that even the physical features about us appear interminable, let alone the invisible immensities. God is not the product of such infinities; He produced them.

Christ is the visible image of the invisible God and He has revealed the otherwise incomprehensible; for no man by searching can find out God. "The secret things belong to the LORD our God; but those things which are revealed belong unto us and to our children forever" (Deut. 29:29). Wherefore our highest knowledge is that we know there are things we cannot know because God has not revealed them. Christ is the full manifestation of Godhead to man, and He brought into our sphere a knowledge of the everlasting God, who saves with an everlasting salvation, who loves with an everlasting love and who adorns His redeemed people with robes of everlasting righteousness, which accompany the gift of everlasting life.

No fewer than twelve of these characteristics that are everlasting are made known in the book of Isaiah the prophet. We also understand that by virtue of His everlastingness, Christ is immune from the limitations of time, and in the immensity of His might He administers through endless ages. ("King of the ages" is the correct rendering in I Timothy 1:17.) By this means also we are able to grasp the fact of the immutability of His will and the immeasurability of His work, together with the incorruptibility of His nature and the immortality of His name. One reason that He is incalculable by our human standards of reckoning is that we have no starting point from whence to begin our investigation.

When Abraham first entered Canaan he found the Amorites were already in the land and that marauding kings were making incursions for purposes of plunder (Gen. 14:1-12). So he was strangely gripped with a sense of the uncertainty and insecurity of the things about him (Gen. 15:1-2). He apparently considered that no real good could come out of setting his mind on possessing a permanent heritage in such a changeful environment. Then the Lord appeared unto Abraham and made with him an everlasting covenant, which immediately prompted his confidence and promoted his trust. He took courage, planted a grove in Beer-Sheba and called there on the name of the Lord, the everlasting God (Gen. 21:33). He had not previously planted anything because of the precariousness of the surroundings.

In a later day King David met with a similar experience in relation to the kingdom of Israel. The Lord appeared to him to reassure his confidence, after which he was able to say, "Yet He hath made with me an everlasting covenant, ordered in all things, and sure" (II Sam. 23:5; also 7:16). Have we been given anything less to stimulate our hope? Listen intently to these words: "Now the God of peace, that brought again from the dead our Lord Jesus, that great shepherd of the sheep, through the blood of the everlasting covenant, make you perfect in every good work to do His will" (Heb. 13:20-21). "He that doeth the will of God abideth for ever" (I John 2:17).

Psalm 90 makes it apparent that Moses also felt the insecurity of life in the wilderness, where he was surrounded by the graves of tens of thousands of slain. This caused him to say, "From everlasting to everlasting, thou art God." In the fact of the eternity of God lay the very foundations of hope. So Moses prayed, "Let the beauty of the LORD our God be upon us: and establish Thou the work of our hands upon us" (Ps. 90:17). How directly and royally his prayer was answered. By the very nature of the request made by Moses, he was actually asking that the immortal beauty and incorruptible glory of the everlasting God, as he had seen it descend on the desert bush (Exod. 3:3) and on the tabernacle (Exod. 40:34-35), may be implanted upon mankind.

Habakkuk the prophet was in a similar dilemma when God gave him to see that the whole of Palestine was to be brought under the domination of Babylon. He cried out in his agony, "Art Thou not from everlasting, O LORD my God, mine Holy One, we shall not die" (Hab. 1:12).

All four of these witnesses — Abraham, David, Moses, Habakkuk—contrast the limitlessness of God and the limitations of man, the boundlessness of Jehovah and the boundaries of mortals, the durability of the Lord and the destructibility of mankind, the permanence of Messiah and the perishing state of humanity.

The One who is everlastingly exquisite in dignified beauty is well able to impart beauty for ashes and to anoint with the oil of joy (Isa. 61:3). He bestows the choicest virtues, the costliest vesture and the comeliest visage on all His beloved people, and garnishes the soul with crystal purity and regal glory forever. "The LORD shall be unto thee an everlasting light" (Isa. 60:19). We are definitely assured of eternal life (John 10:28) and of being partakers of the Divine nature (II Pet. 1:4).

THE EMMANUEL, GOD WITH US

> Behold, a virgin shall be with child, and shall bring forth a son, and they shall call His name Emmanuel, which being interpreted is, God with us (Matt. 1:23).

The disclosure made in this designation describes our Saviour's intimacy with God and His identity with man, which characteristics are combined also with a clear interpretation of the function He came to fulfill. The name gives us a real insight into the character of Christ and the ministry which verifies His claims. "Emmanuel" of the Hebrew language is interpreted in the Greek as "God with us." This at once assures all mankind that the visitation is not limited to the Jewish people, but is a gracious declaration and also an invitation to the Gentile nations as well. This sensational Scriptural name shines out from the very first page of the new covenant to proclaim a real welcome to all burdened or banished souls that care to accept the proposal and come.

This glorious fact is of the highest importance and intentionally intimates the divine interest in humanity. We need not hesitate to emphasize the exceptional reality of this great boon so clearly demonstrated, for since the birth of Christ we have the profoundest proof that God is with us and accessible to all. Whatever may have been the evidences of this previously, and there were many, the coming of Emmanuel ratifies that evidence conclusively.

Everything Christ did was an exhibition of God's power and purpose, everything He said was an expression of God's will and Word, and everything He predicted was an evidence of God's prescience and omniscience. When in attendance at official functions in the temple courts, at all ceremonial services and feasts, and on all occasions of public assemblages for worship, Christ demonstrated the Emmanuel character; and in the person of the Son, God was there. The same was also true in every sphere and in every season, in every association and activity, in every sign given and symbol used. Over the whole range of His teaching and testimony, He set forth the perfect character of God. The Apostle John could say, "No one hath seen God at any time; the only begotten Son, which is in the bosom of the Father, He hath declared Him" (John 1:18).

The Son exhibited the goodness and greatness of God, the grandeur and glory of the Father and the life and love of the Eternal One perfectly. Have we confidence in Jesus as really being God with us? In Him resides the richest resource, from Him reflects the clearest light and on Him remains the truest likeness of Godhead abidingly. Christ in Himself is the sufficiency of God's grace, the infallibility of God's Word, the impregnability of God's peace and the tranquillity of God's rest. Truly in every faculty which He exercised, in every feature which He expressed and in every fact which He emphasized, He exhibited the faithfulness and fullness of God. In the person of Emmanuel all the realities of the unseen are simplified, all revelations of the invisible are unified and all reports of the eternal are clarified. He became to humanity the visible image of the invisible God.

> Amazing thought! Emmanu'l, God with men!
> Such condescension is beyond our ken.
> The glorious God, assumes a human form
> And in our midst the Prince of Peace is born.

We may study the history of the Saviour from a thousand different angles, and each observer from every viewpoint will find He expresses some feature of God. The shepherd sees reflected God's patient care and thoughtful tenderness. The sufferer views the excruciating agony He bore on behalf of others. The sovereign ruler beholds the kingly majesty of His divine sovereignty. The servant recognizes His strenuous labors in ministering to the needy. The steward perceives the trustworthiness of His character. The saint admires the holy deportment of His demeanor in all things. The stranger gazes with rapt attention at the unchanging friendship of His constant love. The stained one observes His cleansing power and purifying truth. The sinner recognizes the kindly tone of His saving appeal and delivering might. The suppliant adores Him for the manifold gifts of His unfailing generosity. The singer considers His utter praise-worthiness and magnifies the beauty of His grace in reverent worship. "God was in Christ, reconciling the world unto Himself." "If I take the wings of the morning, and dwell in the uttermost parts of the sea; even there shall Thy hand lead me, and Thy right hand shall hold me" (Ps. 139:9-10).

THE ENSIGN OF THE PEOPLE

> And in that day there shall be a root of Jesse, which
> shall stand for an ensign of the people; to it shall the
> Gentiles seek: and His rest shall be glorious (Isa. 11:10).

The Person of this prophecy is referred to in the context as
the rod of Jesse and the root of Jesse, the One whom the
Gentiles shall seek after and whose rest shall be glorious. Six
out of the seven occurrences of the word "ensign" used in the
singular number are found in the message of Isaiah the
prophet. A national ensign or flag is held in high regard and is
always displayed on state occasions. So in like manner Christ
will one day become the gathering center for peoples and
nations in a new and unified earth. In hours of national crises
when wars are being waged, standard bearers plant the colors
on the highest eminence and most conspicuous position in the
field of battle, so that all who are engaged in the conflict may
see the symbol of their loyalty to both cause and country.
Although that is so, an ensign is also an office held by those
designated to special tasks in the services of the nation. The
Lord Jesus Christ is officially chosen of God and appointed to
this station, and He is therefore heaven's eternal Ensign for the
world to come, "and unto Him shall the gathering of the
people be" (Gen. 49:10).

The whole of the chapter in which this title occurs is fraught
with great world changes. The control of affairs by local
authorities, provincial governments and national kingdoms is
to be exchanged for one central administration, universal in
its authority and world-wide in its jurisdiction (see Rev.
11:15). When Christ first appeared in manifestation in this
world, the only elevation He received at the hands of man was
the elevation of being uplifted on a brutal cross of shame and
dishonor. Nevertheless His eventual exaltation to pre-
eminence exceeded that of all other principalities and powers
(Eph. 1:21). We are here granted a glimpse into the holiest
purpose ever determined, the biggest project ever decided and
the brightest prospect ever disclosed. "For the earth shall be

full of the knowledge of the LORD, as the waters cover the sea" (Isa. 11:9). This knowledge will prevail universally to the same degree of fullness that we witness in the waters of the expansive ocean. Our blessed Lord will then be manifest as the Ensign in His official capacity and as the global center of attraction, admiration and administration, in "the new earth which I will make" (Isa. 66:22).

Then shall the holy mountain of His majestic reign become the mount of His Messianic rest (v. 10). This is doubtless that rest referred to in Zephaniah 3:17: "The Lord thy God in the midst of thee is mighty; He will save, He will rejoice over thee with joy; He will rest in His love." This is the only verse in Scripture that suggests what the Lord is going to do after He has done all that His infinite love can do.

His inflexible faithfulness and impregnable righteousness assure everything that is essential for an enduring kingdom. Faithfulness portrays a character consistent with itself, a character of unchanging constancy which is wholly reliable. Righteousness indicates a conduct which is incapable of being corrupted in its unvariable conformity to the will of God. These two attributes are intertwined; and in conjoining, form the girdle which binds together the goodness of His grace and the greatness of His glory, so as to stabilize the enactment of His perfect laws.

Let us recall that He holds the highest honor in leadership; He is the most conspicuous in chieftainship. He is the supreme Supervisor of all the services, and He is the capable Commandant who conducts the whole of the campaign which leads to a consummate victory. Never has there been a conqueror who was able to subdue all alien authority, and who was capable of implanting the will of God throughout the world to a degree in which it is done on earth, as it is done in heaven. By the sheer weight of His moral grandeur and spiritual splendor, Christ, as the Ensign of the People outweighs in merit and might the majesty of all other emperors and excellencies. Gorgeously robed in the vesture of virtue, He regains for man the posture of peace and reigns over the new earth in all the pleasure of permanence. His gesture of grace and His leisure of love last uninterruptedly while He interprets to the redeemed the treasures of truth in a measureless ministry which is combined with that holy contentment that is so characteristic of divine culture.

What a distinction! To be high above all principality and power.

What a recognition! To be revered by myriad hosts of men and angels.

What a coronation! To be crowned Lord of lords and King of kings.

What a commemoration! To be admired in all them that believe.

THE EXCELLENCY OF GOD

> The desert shall rejoice, and blossom as the rose. It shall blossom abundantly, and rejoice even with joy and singing: the glory of Lebanon shall be given unto it, the excellency of Carmel and Sharon, they shall see the glory of the LORD, and the excellency of our God (Isa. 35:1-2).

His Excellency is a title of honor given to persons in high office or those holding distinguished rank, and who share the administrative affairs of a kingdom or empire. Frequently the honor is conferred on those who are sent to a foreign country to represent the government of the nation to which they belong. In this same chapter the prophet speaks of the excellency of Carmel and Sharon, a figure which suggests the majestic beauty of the one and the prolific bounty of the other. The true thought of excellency is succinctly expressed in the sublime hymn of Thomas Hastings:

> Majestic sweetness sits enthroned
>   Upon the Saviour's brow;
> His head with radiant glories crowned,
>   His lips with grace o'erflow.
>
> No mortal can with Him compare
>   Among the sons of men;
> Fairer is He than all the fair,
>   Who fill the heavenly train.

On the first occasion this word was used in Scripture, Jacob spoke of "the excellency of dignity, and the excellency of power" that were to pass from Reuben his firstborn who was "unstable as water" (Gen. 49:3-4). But the birthright of the true firstborn abides, and this very chapter supplies four of Christ's Messianic titles: Scepter, Shiloh, Shepherd and Stone.

Moses used the title concerning Jehovah when he wrote the matchless song celebrating the victory over Pharaoh: "In the greatness of Thine excellency Thou hast overthrown them that rose up against Thee" (Exod. 15:7). This is the first of ten songs of praise recorded in the Bible, and its beauty and sublimity ascend to the loftiest heights. Neither Moses, Aaron, Miriam, nor any of the national leaders of Israel appear in it; but the Lord is truly magnified because of His transcendent triumph over oppression and obduracy.

The Lord's excellency is like a great mountain that shuts out all thought of earth, time, space and the powers of man which are so insignificant in comparison. Oh, for a heart to praise and extol the excellency of the Lord Himself! Christ is weightier in His degree of worthiness than all other deliverers. He is statelier in His status of superior strength than any other saviour. He is princelier in His prominence of power and pity than any other protector, and He is courtlier in His command and conquest than any other conqueror. Notice that "Jehovah," rendered "LORD" in the King James version, occurs six times in the first six verses of Moses' song, which concludes with the choice words, "The LORD shall reign for ever and ever" (Exod. 15:18). We should never lose sight of this feature. Salvation is going to culminate in eternal glory (see I Pet. 5:10, 11). Let us prepare for His Excellency a tabernacle of praise, with foundations rooted and grounded deep in love, with pillars of plenteous gratitude, walls of worthy worship, doors of dignified devotion and halls ringing with loud hallelujahs.

Moses, who celebrated the emancipated nation's entrance into the wilderness with a song of victory, commemorated the constancy of the Lord at the close of the march forty years later with another song of triumph (Deut. 32). This chapter is in harmony with the high note of honor which Moses sounded at the beginning of the nation's history. The greatest and grandest glory of Israel is accredited to one cause only, namely, the super-excellence and the sublime perfection of the Saviour who redeemed them from bondage and oppression. Moses remarks that his teaching is to his hearers as the rain, as the dew, as the fine spray and as the showers are to the earth. Within the space of two verses he recounts the memorable name, the majestic greatness, the matchless character, the marvelous work, the manifold ways, the multiform truth and the munificent attributes of their gracious Guide, glorious Guardian and generous Governor (Deut. 32:3-4). No wonder he goes on to call this Saviour of Israel, "the sword of thy excellency" (Deut. 33:29).

He who is named the excellency of Jacob in Psalm 47:4 is the one who pledges to make Zion "an eternal excellency" (Isa. 60:15). "When He shall appear, we shall be like Him" (I John 3:2). Christ, in keeping with His own character, is arrayed "in majesty and excellency" and in "glory and beauty" (Job 40:10). He stands alone throughout the ages without equal and without rival, excelling all and exceeding all. The Epistle to the Hebrews directs our attention to His more excellent name, His more excellent ministry and His more excellent sacrifice.

The evidences of His excellency are fully expressed during His earthly ministry. For verification we may examine His faithful constancy, His friendly courtesy, His fearless chivalry and His faultless consistency. As the Representative of the Father of glory, His high rank and holy resemblance warrant our speaking of Him as, "His Excellency Christ Jesus the Lord." This is He who adorns greatness, garnishes graciousness, beautifies goodness and gilds glory. His celestial comeliness and complete constancy are credentials possessed by no other celebrity. Our Lord's utterances supersede the statements made by the world's most famous orators and statesmen and His name is excellent in all the earth. The striking argument presented in this Psalm of Messiah, Psalm 8, is that He has the absolute right to ascend the throne of the universe as Lord of the whole earth; firstly by virtue of His adorable excellence and secondly because of His amazing love in redeeming at infinite cost so insignificant a creature as man.

THE ETERNAL GOD

> There is none like unto the God of Jeshurun, who rideth upon the heaven in thy help, and in His excellency on the sky. The eternal God is thy refuge, and underneath are the everlasting arms . . . . Israel then shall dwell in safety alone . . . . Happy art thou, O Israel: who is like unto thee, O people saved by the LORD (Deut. 33:26-29).

The first use of the word "eternal" in the Bible is associated with God as being our refuge. Seeing that this steadfast expression of abidingness is attached to our secure hiding place we need have no doubt about the degree and duration of our deliverance. The gift of life, the grace of love and the glory of light which Christ brings to us are all eternal and in harmony with His own character. What ecstasy of joy should enrich our lives as we engage in contemplating our eternal Redeemer and the desirability of His redemption. How marvelous it is to realize that a divine Person is our Protector, our Preserver and our Provider. He Himself is of nobler worth than the wealth of blessing He bestows. He is far more precious than the privilege of participation in an incorruptible inheritance which He bequeaths. His dignified character is of greater consideration than the costly treasures He confers. Moreover, His friendship, fellowship and faithfulness are likewise eternal, together with His majestic power and His matchless purpose (Rom. 1:20; Eph. 3:11). The same is true of His great salvation and His gracious Spirit (Heb. 5:9; 9:14), and in thirty passages in the New Testament "eternal" qualifies the life Christ imparts to the believing soul.

By virtue of His being the Eternal God, time cannot tarnish the trophies of His triumph, decades cannot diminish the dignity of His dominion, ages cannot alter the achievements of

His ability, centuries cannot canker the character of His constancy, aeons cannot atrophy the administration of His authority, epochs cannot enervate the exercise of His energy, periods cannot paralyze the prevailing of His purpose and millenniums cannot mar the ministry of His mediation. With such wonderful assurances given, we are persuaded that no duration, whatever its dimension, can destroy the defenses of our security, because the Eternal God is our refuge.

One version has rendered the words of the title passage, "The eternal God is thy abode." This translation reminds us that when Christ was manifest, He repeatedly uttered the words, "Abide in Me." These words convey nothing less than the assurance of eternal companionship. What regal association is this, what royal accommodation, yea, and what real animation!

In addition to the Eternal One being our refuge, underneath are the everlasting arms, which assures us adequately that the foundations are secure and sound. The seven pillars of wisdom support this dwelling place (Prov. 9:1). We are therefore undergirded by the unlimited power of a steadfast Friend and cannot be undermined by even the untiring persistence of a subtle foe. When Satan desired to put Peter through the sieve, how graciously Christ safeguarded him from despair. If we are assailed, attacked or accused we have the everlasting arms to hold us and the eternal abiding place to hide us. The Prophet Isaiah may have been directed by the Spirit of God to this very description of defense wherein we are both held and hidden when He wrote the words, "Thou wilt keep him in perfect peace, whose mind is stayed on Thee: because he trusteth in Thee. Trust ye in the Lord for ever: for in the Lord Jehovah is everlasting strength. . . . Come, my people, enter thou into thy chambers. . .hide thyself as it were for a little moment" (Isa. 26:3-4,20).

The immovable arches of immortal love have spanned the abysmal chasms of darkness beneath. Now we are assured of the innumerable blessings of sustaining strength and shielding sympathy in Him. Christ is the source of supply and secret of sufficiency of all sustenance for spiritual life. So the eternal

God gives us the assurance of this and He will never let us down. His pledges are not fine weather favors that flourish amid calmness and prove flimsy in the fierceness of battle. We find a weighty demonstration of His sustaining strength in relation to this very earth which He hung upon nothing (Job 26:7), which He founded upon the seas and established upon the floods (Ps. 24:2; see also II Pet. 3:5-7). So likewise of Zion it is stated, "The highest Himself shall establish her" (Ps. 87:5). "As the mountains are round about Jerusalem, so the Lord is round about His people from henceforth even for ever" (Ps. 125:2).

In view of such things, should any be called upon to face depths of grief that are unfathomable, dangers that are insuperable, or darkness that is impenetrable or a dilemma that is unsolvable, or a disease that is incurable, or duties that are undesirable, or a district of service that is uninhabitable, remember He is immutable and His everlasting arms are underneath.

> Surrounded by God, encircled with love,
> His arms are beneath, His eye is above,
> A rearward behind me, a Leader before,
> He dwelleth within me, so what need I more?

THE ENGRAVER OF THE NAME

> Zion said, The LORD hath forsaken me, and my Lord hath forgotten me. Can a woman forget her sucking child, that she should not have compassion on the son of her womb? yea, they may forget, yet will I not forget thee. Behold, I have graven thee upon the palms of My hands (Isa. 49:15-16).

When the Lord uses "behold," it is sufficient to indicate that something startling is to follow. In this instance we stand astonished at the declaration that is made. Listen to the music of the words, "Behold, I have graven thee on the palms of My hands." I, the Architect and Artist of the ages, the Designer of the everlasting habitations, "I have graven thee." A ring of reality sounds forth from this statement, reminding us of other utterances equally exciting: "I have chosen," "I have called," "I have made," "I have given" and such like, all of which we cherish dearly. No indefiniteness marks the words such as marks "I may," "I might," or "I must." Whatever else may happen to other engravings on stone or steel, in this case no erasure is feasible because He is immortal, and no error is possible because He is immutable. None can efface the engraving because He dwelleth in light which no man can approach. What antiquity is attached to the engraving of the Ancient of Days, as compared with the deep-cut hieroglyphics of the basalt rocks of Egypt. Even before the days of earth's earliest infancy, or ever she had burst her swaddling bands of cloudy mist; prior to the shooting forth of effulgent sun rays across the bosom of the sky; preceding the peeping of stars with twinkling eyes athwart the cerulean arch; the Eternal had focused His heart's love on His ransomed society and fastened the remembrance of His loved object on the palms of His hands. Not written, stamped or printed on pages of parchment is this name, but graven forevermore.

The suggestiveness of the figure expresses eternal election; it indicates inseverable identity; it intimates an ineffable immortality; yea, the very fashion of its design foretells an unending union with an incomparable Lover. No human merit can induce Christ to engrave the name and no human monarch can insist on its being done. Philanthropists, potentates, principalities and philosophers have no influence here, not even enough to have one single name inscribed in such a place. The sole prerogative is according to the riches of His grace, and according to the good pleasure of His will. The endorsement of His everlasting love is the only recommendation needed; the endearment of His affectionate heart of infinite mercy is the sole commendation to assure the graving of the name on the palms of His hands.

The lines that are imprinted on our hands at birth remain unchanged until our burial at death. But God has no birth or burial, so the engraving on His hands remains forever. These are the hands wherewith He wrought the mighty wonders of creation, all the features of which creation were designed by the wealth of His wisdom. These are the same hands which have been guiding, guarding and governing through the centuries, but never before was it known that both palms were memorial tablets.

To be engraven on His hands is expressive of the favor of a faithful Guardian and likewise it exhibits a distinctive honor bestowed by a powerful Governor. We learn from these things how precious the Church is to Christ, how desirous He is to honor her, how generous He is in her favor and how vigorous His ministry of intercession whereby He assures to His Bride ineffable splendor. No fondness has ever been expressed to any loved favorite in this world that is comparable to the favor Christ has shown to His people (Ps. 106:4-5). We may esteem this act as one of the marvels of His ministry, we may count it among the miracles of His mercy and we may accept it as one of the great mysteries of His monarchy.

> Our name is engraven upon His own hands,
> Our witness in heaven eternally stands;
> The nearest and dearest and choicest to Him,
> Without spot or wrinkle without or within.
> The tables and tablets of brass and of stone
> With their deeply cut letters are soon overthrown;
> But none can erase the indelible names
> Of those He redeems and eternally claims.

THE ESTIMATOR OF VALUES

> Now when He had left speaking He said unto Simon,
> Launch out into the deep, and let down your nets for a
> draught. And Simon answering said unto Him, Epistata,
> we have toiled all night and have taken nothing:
> nevertheless at Thy word I will let down the net (Luke
> 5:4-5).

> The priest shall estimate it, whether it be good or bad:
> as the priest shall estimate it, so shall it stand (Lev.
> 27:14).

The title, Epistata, which is rendered in our English version
by the word "master," is used on seven occasions in Luke's
Gospel and means to be set over, to estimate, or appraise. In
the chapter quoted from the Book of Leviticus the function of
valuing and appraising was committed to Moses and the
priesthood. The word "estimation" is used there twenty-six
times. This duty of estimating was strictly carried out and
performed according to the standard value of the shekel of the
sanctuary. God reserved to Himself the sole right of estimating
the value of all things to which He was entitled. In like manner
our Lord Jesus Christ, who emancipates from the burden and
thraldom of sin as a strong and sufficient Saviour, expects in
return the loyalty of our love and labor. In whatever we may
engage, or whatsoever we devote to Him of time, talent or
treasure, He reserves to Himself the right of judging its value.

In the case of Simon Peter, Christ had requested the use of
his boat at a time of emergency, when the people thronged to
hear the Word of God (Luke 5:1-3). Simon had responded,
and Christ intended to suitably recompense him for the time
spent and for the use of the fishing-craft. So when He had
finished speaking to the people, Christ told Simon to launch
out into the deep and to let down the nets for a catch. The
experienced fisherman did not appreciate the order, and more
so, after a night of fruitless toil. Simon expressed himself quite
frankly, but added, "Nevertheless at Thy word I will let down
a net." Then suddenly the simple action became sublimely

great; for a great multitude of fish was taken (v. 6). Simon obeyed this greatest of all powers in the universe, which is "Thy Word." The Word of the Lord holds fabulous stars in their courses; and, the marvel of it all, swimming fish obey the same law as the spinning spheres. Simon used the title, Epistata, *not knowing what he said.* Christ assumed the responsibility of the title immediately, assessed the value of Simon Peter's obedient response and furnished him with two boatloads of fish in recompense for the use of his fishing craft.

Christ has a correct estimate of all labor; He knows the true value of any gift of time, energy or money we devote to Christian work or workers. His word is the final court of appeal; He decides accurately, perfectly and finally on all matters of spiritual energy, endowment and experience. The Lord knows far more about the fishing, farming and fruitgrowing industries than we do.

Over and beyond the physical sphere, He it is who estimates the worth of our worship, He records the value of our virtue, He weighs the worthiness of our work and appraises the amount of our reward for faithful activities. Yea, He determines the depth and degree of our devotion, He reckons with rectitude the recompense deserved and He places His price on the presentation of our praise. He has a better insight into the character of Paul's service at Corinth than any of the philosophers, merchants and scholars of that city. Christ knows the quality of our endurance, the motive of our obedience and the measure of our confidence. He is fully aware of every man's endowment, environment and of the energy exerted in every endeavor made to do the will of God. Such things He has plainly and lucidly expressed in His illustrations regarding the three parables about money — the pounds, the pence and the talents. No one can vie with Him as a valuator, no one can compare with Him as an appraiser and no one can equal Him as an estimator; therefore He brooks no intrusion of others in this realm and will not permit the interference of any would-be judges.

In the finest hour of the life of Mary of Bethany, when the keen penetration of her sensitive love looked and beheld something the disciples failed to perceive, she arose and a few moments later advanced toward her Messiah with an alabaster box of costly spikenard and anointed Him. She entered with Him into the holiest court of sorrow and touched the hem of His garment of sacrifice, not to gain a benefit but to give her best. Judas Iscariot straightway intruded an estimate of her act, but Christ sternly rebuked him and said, "Let her alone . . . she is come aforehand to anoint My body to the burying" (Mark 14:6-8). Judas did not know that Mary had held back the ointment from being used on her brother Lazarus who had died a week before. She had kept it for Him. He immediately places His own estimate on her deed, saying, "Wheresoever this gospel shall be preached throughout the whole world, this also that she hath done shall be spoken of for a memorial of her" (v. 9). What appreciation! Christ is the only One that can lift spiritual devotion into world-wide recognition. Jochabed the mother of Moses was abundantly rewarded for risking her life to save her child. Cornelius also had noticeable recognition taken of his prayers and generosity (Acts 10:31).

Christ, who is perfect in His appreciation, reserves to Himself the exclusive right of estimating the worth of everything to which He is entitled, according to His own standards of righteous valuation. He has the sharpest eye and keenest insight; nothing escapes His observation whether it be done in acts of liberality, hospitality, loyalty or sympathy; and He will not entrust this sacred function to any other. We are, each of us, personally responsible to Him for what we do; each one is accountable to the overseeing Valuer and Appraiser who passes unerring estimates on all features of His people's work.

THE ESTABLISHER OF COVENANTS

> With thee will I establish My covenant; and thou shalt come into the ark, thou, and thy sons, and thy wife, and thy sons' wives with thee (Gen. 6:18).

> And I, behold, I establish My covenant with you, and with your seed after you (9:9).

Noah was not in possession of a volume of Scripture to direct his steps as we are, but God revealed Himself to the patriarch and established a covenant with him to make known the divine line of activity which the Lord intended to take in His dealings with the earth and its inhabitants. This was really necessary, after the unprecedented flood had taken place, to instill confidence into the hearts of those who were to replenish the earth. The Lord in establishing this covenant made it to be co-existent with light, as He so purposefully displayed in the rainbow sign: "I do set My bow in the cloud" (Gen. 9:13).

This symbol is highly significant and stands as a conspicuous fingerpost directing our attention to One who is the covenant (Isa. 42:6). Christ did declare during His ministry, "I am the light of the world" (John 8:12). So Messiah is not merely the Messenger of the covenant (Mal. 3:1), and the Mediator of a better covenant (Heb. 8:6), and the Maker of the covenant (Heb. 10:16), but He is Himself the covenant (Isa. 49:8). In all His pulsating sympathy, personal suitability, and as our precious surety, He is at once the Maintainer of all that the covenant involves.

We are dealing with a Christ who is God's possession and ours. Because He is inscrutable in wisdom, insuperable in power, inflexible in justice, inseparable in love, invulnerable in constancy, infallible in truth, invincible in might and immutable in will, we possess in Him an everlasting covenant. Each of us is privileged to say of this immortal One, "My beloved is mine, and I am his" (S. of Sol. 2:16). This is not only true of the mighty salvation He secures and the memorable agreement He settles, but His prescience, prudence and providence involved in the great transaction are also mine. He "offered Himself without spot to God" (Heb. 9:14), He "gave Himself for me" (Gal. 2:20). As Son of God, Son of man, Arm of the Lord and Holy One of God, He is mine and I am His. The whole Christ, the sum and substance of purity, integrity, fidelity and constancy, is mine. The majesty as King of kings, the authority as Lord of lords, the sanctuary as the Heaven of heavens and the transcendency as the Name of names are His; and He is mine.

What a crown of credit and miter of merit belong to Him as the king-priest, how honorable He has been in establishing the will and testament, how dependable in confirming the contract, how reliable in achieving agreement and how adorable in ascending to the right hand of the Majesty on high to assure acceptance. He is so spotless in His beauty, so peerless in His glory and so stainless in His sanctity that everything connected with Him is everlasting. This pertains to the lovingkindness of His heart, the righteousness of His will, the perfectness of His ways, the preciousness of His mind and the holiness of His character. How could He be anything else than everlasting as the covenant?

Moreover, Christ as our great High Priest has our names graven in His breastplate, shoulder pieces and hand palms for a memorial. These figures indicate firstly the place of gracious sympathy, the affection of His heart, where we are represented in the deep-cut jewels of the Urim and the Thummim. Secondly, the place of governmental authority, the shoulders of honor, whereon rest the government and peace without end (Isa. 9:6). Thirdly, the glorious ability, the almightiness of His hand, which sways the sovereign scepter of everlasting strength. By covenant right we are identified with the sympathy, stability and sovereignty of Messiah's everlasting glory.

Have we the conviction that His pledges are true? Anything of divine authorship abides. He has authorized the forgiveness of sins, therefore it will not suffer frustration. He has confirmed the compact; there cannot be any cancellation. He has ratified the covenant; revocation is impossible. We are entitled to enter into the enjoyment of what these realities entail. The name He bears, the fame He shares and the crown He wears comprise a portion of our riches in glory by Christ Jesus. The thought of these things should enlighten the mind, transport the soul and ravish the heart of every true believer.

THE EXECUTOR OF JUDGMENT

For as the Father hath life in Himself; so hath He given to the Son to have life in Himself; and hath given Him authority to execute judgment also, because He is the Son of Man (John 5:26, 27).

Whose hope is in the LORD his God: which made heaven, and earth . . . which keepeth truth for ever: which executeth judgment for the oppressed (Ps. 146:5-7).

The judicial grandeur of Christ in His capacity as Judge contributes an additional splendor to the stately array of His perfect abilities and attributes. The high court of justice in the heavens infinitely exceeds in dignity and solemnity all the tribunals of earthly adjudicature. This dignified office should awaken our wonder and arouse us to an adoring attitude of worship. He who appeared in human form and was found in fashion as a man is well versed in all the frailties of life on earth. As the Man of Sorrows He knows what it is to suffer and to serve in submissive obedience. He encountered the supremest form of temptation and trouble that assail the soul and endured the greatest contradiction of sinners against Himself. No one else than He is more qualified to execute judgment. He went surety for debtors in their destitution when all were hopelessly bankrupt, in order to make them solvent, and experienced at the time the extremes of hunger and thirst.

Challenged as to His claims at the close of His ministry, in the most critical hour of crisis, when treachery betrayed Him, instability denied Him, timidity deserted Him, carnality despised Him, enmity derided Him, profanity mocked Him and obduracy disdained Him, He did not relinquish His stand, but declared emphatically before the high priest that he would one day see the Son of man sitting on the right hand of power (Matt. 26:64). He made this astounding claim before Caiaphas when outward appearances did not assure it, existing evidences did not endorse it, surrounding circumstances did not corroborate it, nor did local conditions confirm it any wise; yet He was wholly unperturbed and undaunted by the derision of the people. Our Lord described the tidings of terror that would grip mankind, and said that amid shaking spheres, the wreck of worlds and the crash of creation He would appear on His throne to judge all nations. We gather from the vivid description He gave that His array of power and glory at the last and grand assize will be awesome in its surpassing splendor.

Christ fully knows what the degenerate heart is capable of expressing at its worst, as well as what the regenerate life is capable of expressing at its best. How befitting that He who encountered the extremest execrations of enmity from humanity should be the sole Executor of judgment in the celestial court of justice. He knows what is in the heart of all men, and requires no witness to supply evidence (John 2:24-25). Christ clearly explained in His teaching that everyone would be called to face His tribunal (John 5:25-29). He declared that His cross would be the deciding factor of condemnation or justification (John 12:31-33). The final unveiling verifies His great claim, for He is presented as the sole Executor of judgment (Rev. 14:14-16; 20:11-14).

So then as Arbiter and Adjudicator Christ possesses credentials that are complete; He exercises powers of perception and comprehension that are perfect; wherefore His verdicts and sentences are absolute and final. He was confident His word would win the ultimate victory, that His majesty would mature in magnificence and triumph gloriously and that His pre-eminent power would prevail universally.

THE ELECT SERVANT

> Behold My servant, whom I uphold; Mine elect, in
> whom My soul delighteth; I have put My spirit upon
> Him; He shall bring forth judgment to the Gentiles. . . .
> He shall not fail nor be discouraged, till He have set
> judgment in the earth (Isa. 42:1-4).

In the preceding chapter this prophet of God proclaims the
noticeable absence of notable national leaders among the
people. After a careful investigation of the kingdom for a
competent counsellor who had ability to foresee coming events
and frame a suitable policy in the light of the forecast, not one
was found (41:28). In contrast to this deplorable state of
deficiency, the divine declaration is made concerning One
who is fully acquainted with local conditions and who also has
a clear conception of the course future events will take.
"Behold My servant . . . Mine elect." No matter what may be
the degree of excellence attained by earthly leaders, their
efficiency continues but a short time and death ends their
enterprise and effectiveness without either stability or finality
being reached. This is not the case with God's Elect, who by
heavenly choice is assigned a pre-eminent office and by highest
consent is appointed to permanent oversight.

He is none other than the ascended Redeemer and anointed
Regent, who is replete in resource and resolute in
righteousness. His prescience enables Him to prepare for every
eventuality and His providence provides for every emergency.
By virtue of the insight of His inherent wisdom and the insistence of His immutable will, His work of administration
abides forever. He must prevail because He is upheld by divine
omnipotence and possesses the power to subdue all things unto
Himself. He is capable of cleansing His kingdom of all things
that offend (Matt. 13:41).

Do we doubt His durability, do we deem it possible that He
shall one day be deflected from His program and be defeated
in His purpose? Take heed then to the clear divine
declaration: "He shall not fail" (Isa. 42:4), and notice also the
twelve "I wills" of authoritative determination which occur in

Isaiah 42. If we also consider the imposing selection of
Jehovah: "I the Lord have called thee in righteousness" (v. 6);
the anointing of the insuperable Spirit: "I have put My spirit
upon Him" (v.1); and the capability of the invincible servant:
"Behold My servant . . . Mine elect" (v. 1); then the strongest
reassurance imaginable will burst upon the soul. This thrice-
famous One foresees all the future, forestalls the formidable
foe and from His unbounded resource furnishes His forces
with a rare fortitude that enables them to face the fray
triumphantly (Acts 4:13).

How amazing that the Lord of all should become Servant of
all, and that He who was stately in His supremacy should bow
down to become Surety and Substitute for strangers and
sinners. The wonderful Counsellor becomes the watchful
Caretaker, the marvelous Sovereign becomes the merciful
Shepherd, the glorious Master becomes the gracious Minister
and the omnipotent Superior becomes the obedient Servant.
As a Servant He must succeed because of His background
(Phil. 2:6-7). How is it possible for Jehovah's Servant-Elect,
who is assigned a stewardship of such proportions, ever to be
defeated? Behind His character and commission stands the
dignity of His sonship, the reality of His heirship, the
supremacy of His headship, the maturity of His judgeship, the
ability of His governorship, the majesty of His kingship and
the authority of His lordship.

We find it difficult for our minds to keep in focus at one and
the same time both the loftiness and lowliness, the holiest and
humblest characteristics that are so perfectly embodied in
Christ. We find it hard to link Jehovah-nissi and Jesus of
Nazareth and to perceive the glory of deity reflected in
humanity. How frequently we are told in the message of
Hebrews to consider Him; for if we attentively observe His
demeanor in service, we shall see how boldy he faced the
staggering task with resolute step, deliberate fortitude and
confident assurance. Can we wonder at His succeeding in the
mighty plan of planting justice and equity in the earth? Duty
demanded of Him, among other things, that He should
displace disruption and deceit and ensure law, depose

darkness and enthrone light, defeat deviltry and enshrine love, destroy death and establish life. Who but He is sufficient for such things?

He veiled the splendor of His superior dignity and voluntarily ventured into the path of strenuous duty as the Elect Servant. By virtue of undertaking the prodigious project He redeems the world from ruination, re-establishes the work of righteousness (Isa. 32:16-19), reduces all contending rivalries (Isa. 24:21), regenerates man and reconciles all things to God, replenishes truth and justice (Isa. 42:4), rules in equity and reigns in regal majesty forever (Isa. 32:1-2).

The monstrous image of unrighteousness that had gripped the world in Daniel's vision and filled the earth with violence and corruption was too big a proposition for man to cope with. A stone cut out without hands was necessary, an instrument independent of human energy and endeavor was the only hope and source of help. The weapons of this warfare were not carnal, for the Elect Servant wielded truth divinely strong, love steadfastly true, sinlessness profoundly brave, meekness helpfully kind, peace attractively calm and grace impartially free.

Such a Servant is never baffled by subtlety nor beaten by superiority; He cannot be blinded with bribes nor bought over with flatteries; and He will never be defeated by pleasures nor discouraged by problems. If we stop to table all the facts and examine the great undertaking, how noble the sight we gain, how able the Servant we see, how stable the work that He does, and how creditable the triumph He wins.

When we consider the frailty of much of the material He has to work on, including such undesirables as smoking flax, which is so nauseous, and such unreliables as bruised reeds, which are such a nuisance, we may well wonder why He does not falter. The first appear worthless, while the second group represents weakness itself. We should remember there is a definite reason why He does not faint and become discouraged. His very submission to infinite power assures unlimited ability; therefore this unusual Potter can regenerate and remake the marred vessels.

He has already demonstrated in the material realm that He can change clay into sapphire, transform graphite into diamond, transfigure grains of grit or disease germs in oysters into pearls, sift the finest particles of dust through the finest of porous rock in moisture and produce the colorful opal. He is able to transmute a common chrysalis into a beautiful butterfly, turn raindrops into snowflakes and water into wine, and is never baffled nor beaten in any work He begins (Phil. 1:6). He shall not fail, He will not fail, He cannot fail until He brings forth judgment unto victory (Isa. 42:3). Wherefore failure is not final; what He commences He consummates. Here is One who can bring a clean thing out of an unclean in contradiction of Job 14:4. He produces life out of death as in the case of the beautiful ichneumon fly from a corrupting carcass. He restores the years which the canker worm hath eaten, He mends the song bird's broken wing and He receives, reclothes and reinstates the prodigal in righteousness forever.

"He shall bring forth judgment to the Gentiles" (Isa. 42:1).

"He shall bring forth judgment unto victory" (v. 3, R.V.).

"He shall not fail . . . till He have set judgment in the earth" (v. 4).

"Sing unto the LORD a new song, and His praise from the end of the earth" (v. 10).

"The LORD is well pleased for His righteousness' sake; He will magnify the law, and make it honourable" (v. 21).

THE EXPRESS IMAGE

> Who being the brightness of His glory, and the express image of His person, and upholding all things by the word of His power, when He had by Himself purged our sins, sat down on the right hand of the Majesty on high (Heb. 1:3).

This is one of the most vital truths taught in the Scriptures. Christ replaces infinite silence with speech, and those celestial realities which at one time were closely concealed from mankind are now through Him clearly revealed. The obscure has been made obvious, and the deepest mysteries have been divinely manifested. The exact expression of the Eternal One is exhibited in the person of the Son. He is much more than a semblance; He constitutes the very subsistence of Godhead. Here we are brought into actual contact with the reality of the hypostatic union which ever exists between Father and Son. Christ is the Express Image, not an emanation but very essence of and the exact replica of Deity, yea the visible image of the invisible God.

Therefore, during His earthly ministry and manifestation, our Lord was able to say assuredly, "He that hath seen Me hath seen the Father." "I and My Father are one" (John 14:9; 10:30). In corroboration of this clear witness, we have the testimony of the Apostle John, "The only begotten Son, which is in the bosom of the Father, He hath declared Him" (John 1:18). The greatest witness relative to this matter comes from heaven itself, "This is My beloved Son, in whom I am well pleased" (Matt. 3:17). The Father's love rests upon the Son with unabated fullness and is reciprocated fully and perfectly. We ascertain from revealed truth that in holiness of personality, in harmony of purpose and in heavenly prerogative, Father and Son are one (John 17:21-22).

The Son expresses the Father completely in resembling His excellent wisdom, in representing in exercise His essential will and in revealing His exquisite worthiness. Christ fully expresses the goodness of God's nature, He faithfully exhibits the grace of God's nobility and finally explains the glory of God's name. So then because of His absolute and abiding likeness, in loveliness there is no difference, and in loving kindness there is no divergence in form (Phil. 2:6).

When a gold seal is impressed on softened wax the image left corresponds exactly to the seal itself, but the wax consists of an entirely different substance and is of a much lesser value than the gold. In the instance of Christ's being the Express Image of God, the matter greatly differs; for both Father and Son are the same in subsistence and they are wholly alike in mind, will and heart. In other words, the intellectual, volitional and emotional attributes agree in one.

Thou art the everlasting Word, the Father's only Son,
God manifestly seen and heard, and Heaven's beloved One.
True Image of the Infinite whose essence is concealed,
Brightness of uncreated light, the heart of God revealed.

In the truest sense of the word, Christ is actually the Father's signet by whom all divine proclamations are sealed; for the word "signet" is derived from the root "to seal." The Father implants upon the Son His own seal, so that Christ is the very imprint of the Most High (John 6:27). We may find a figure of this in the Old Testament in the instance of the Lord's choosing Zerubbabel to be His signet (Haggai 2:23). Wherever this man went he left behind an impression for God. Christ in manifestation is God's signet. Wherever He went and in whatsoever He wrought, He demonstrated Godlikeness, to the glory of God the Father. Our Lord Jesus Christ is the Express Image of the Father's infinite foreknowledge, His inestimable fullness, intrinsic faithfulness and of His intimate friendship.

The moral grandeur and spiritual splendor of Christ outvies to an infinite degree the glories of the supreme potentates of time. The One who exhibits the express image of the Eternal is the same also who declares and displays every feature of resemblance and resplendence in heavenly relationship. He willed and worked in the power of the immutable and incorruptible character of creatorship. He loved and labored with the clearest intellectual insight and insistence of suretyship for the reconciling of all things unto Himself (II Cor. 5:19; Col. 1:20-21). He taught and wrought in the fullest consciousness and confidence of Messiahship (John 4:25-26). He pledged and proved the constancy of fidelity and faithfulness in friendship (John 15:14-15). He defended and delivered God's people with all the protection and perfection of guardianship (John 17:12). He bore every insignia of perfect regality and royalty in kingship. Yea, in his empowerment, His endowment and enthronement He altogether transcends. Without controversy, Christ is "the express image of His person." What a vocation! What a varisemblance! What a verification!

THE END

> And He said unto me, It is done. I am Alpha and
> Omega, the beginning and the end (Rev. 21:6).

How self-revealing this title is of the self-existing One, who is
the goal and objective of all creation. The name sets forth the
indestructibility and incorruptibility of Him who bears it as a
designation of dignity and durability. Christ holds many titles
that no other being could even attempt to adopt. How truly
befitting this is, that He who is the Originator of all things
visible, should also be their Terminator.

But the name means much more than being the terminator
of this temporal and transient system of things. Christ is the
End or aim for which all things are created; He is their sole
End and ultimate objective: "for Thy pleasure they are and
were created" (Rev. 4:11). As the End, He outlives and
outlasts all other celebrities, He overcomes all opposition to
the will of God and oversees the establishment of the divine
will in the new order of the fullness of times (Eph. 1:9-10).
Christ is certainly going to end all rejection of that will
throughout the entire universe (I Cor. 15:25). No power that
opposes His almightiness can finally prevail because He is
unvariable; no hour can ever arise when He will be taken at a
disadvantage. He has already supervised the historic ages from
the very start; He has sustained the universe since its beginning
and will continue to superintend until the ultimate issue, when
all things shall be diverted to the fulfilling of His eternal
purpose.

This name is like a tiny key that unlocks a formidable
treasury glistening with wealth. "End" is only a tiny term, but
it turns our attention to ever broadening regions of truth and
reminds us of the American Standard Version of Psalm 16:2,
"Thou art my LORD: I have no good beyond Thee." *Ne plus
ultra,* no more beyond, no more of quest for good or zest in
toil. Eureka! Having found Him of whom Moses in the law and
the prophets wrote, we have reached the end of desire, the
goal of good, the climax of hope; so from henceforth our only

outlook is Christ, *plus ultra,* evermore beyond. For this is He of whom it is written, "Of Him, and through Him, and to Him, are all things: to whom be glory forever. Amen (Rom. 11:36).

Everything is out of gear and without a guiding hand if this objective be not in view; for everything here is partial; "but when that which is perfect is come, then that which is in part shall be done away" (I Cor. 13:10). Apart from Christ, law has no project (Rom. 10:4), life has no purpose (Rom. 14:8, 9), labor has no prospect (Col. 3:17) and love has no prize. If permanent joy is sought, let every butterfly of pleasure alight upon this fragrant flower of the heart, the Rose of Sharon, or nestle close beside this blessed bloom of the bosom, the Lily of the Valleys. Only in Him can perfect bliss be found.

The Jews had many things of value: the sonship (Exod. 4:22), the glory, the covenants, the law, the promises, etc. (Rom. 9:4, 5); but they missed the End, the very goal toward which their whole sacrificial and sacerdotal system directed. Amid a setting of remarkable realities, which culminate in the supremacy of Christ, the Apostle Paul declares, "Then cometh the end, when He shall have delivered up the kingdom to God, even the Father; when He shall have put down all rule and authority and power . . . the last enemy that shall be destroyed is death" (I Cor. 15:24,26). In the chapter the apostle portrays the most glorious deeds, the grandest triumphs and the greatest splendors that pertain to our Lord and Saviour in relation to final issues.

The use made of "end" in the New Testament is significant. The meaning indicates an issue, fulfillment, consummation, maturity and uttermost of a system or order of things, in the light of which Christ is the supreme objective, the final goal, the topmost aim, the ultimate purpose and uttermost issue of all things. Both the issue of sin and the issue of faith are stated in Romans 6:21-22. In that same sense Christ is the issue of this transient world. He will end the stormy winds, the chilling blasts, the stifling heat, the sobbing cries, the stinging blows and the stunning words. All such conflicts cease forever. Yea, He terminates trials and tears, He stills squalls and storms, He stops sighs and sobs, He finishes foes and fears, He quells quarrels and quips, He concludes conflicts and cares and He ends envies and evils. He makes final forever all that defiles and defies, and will destroy the last enemy.

Then we shall see the things which cannot be shaken remaining forever. Truth abides, virtue survives, love lives, peace persists, righteousness rules, joy continues and friendly fellowship flourishes eternally. Change, force, time and space, the four separating factors we know so well here, will not be able to sever us from His love over there (Rom. 8:38-39). His own self-existence is without beginning or boundary, His holiness knows no hem or horizon, His features are free from furrows and fatigue, His beauty knows no blur nor blemish, His sympathy is without score or shore, and we shall be like Him who is the living sunshine of the nightless day (Rev. 21:23).

Not only is He the End in relation to this temporal system, but He is the main object and objective in the new order.

F

The titanic capacities and canyon-like capabilities that are indicated by Christ's names and nature surpass the entire range of all human standards of calculation and reckoning.

The FIRSTBORN (Rom. 8:29)
> Unrivaled in resplendence, foremost in honor.

The FORERUNNER (Heb. 6:20)
> The File-leader, triumphant and stately.

The FIRSTFRUITS (I Cor. 15:20)
> Vitally competent and vigorously constant.

The FAITHFUL ONE (Rev. 3:14)
> The essence and expression of eternal Truth.

The FOUNTAIN OF LIFE (Ps. 36:9)
> The spring and source of full satifaction.

The FOUNDATION (I Cor. 3:11)
> The permanence of replete righteousness.

The FAIRER THAN MEN (Ps. 45:2)
> His beauty never blemishes.

The FRIEND OF SINNERS (Luke 7:34)
> The trustworthy Helper who never fails.

The FELLOW OF GOD (Zech. 13:7)
> His mutual affinity in purpose and power.

The FIRST (Rev. 1:11)
> The Lord's solitary grandeur.

The FULLNESS OF GODHEAD (Col. 2:9)
> The manifold magnitude of Messiah's resource.

The FORGIVER OF SINS (Luke 5:20)
> Handsome in the dignity of His pardoning grace.

IN HIM DWELLETH

ALL THE FULLNESS OF GODHEAD BODILY

Christ is mightiest in majesty
Christ is strongest in sovereignty
Christ is ablest in authority
Christ is choicest in constancy
Christ is chiefest in capability
Christ is greatest in generosity
Christ is stateliest in supremacy

IN WHOM ARE HID ALL

THE TREASURES OF WISDOM

The First and Foremost of all ranks,
The Friend to whom we all give thanks
The Gracious Master who forgives,
And all that mars the soul outlives.

Rich crowns and diadems adorn
The brow once pierced with cruel thorn,
And Heaven's honors glorify
The Lamb who came to earth to die.

No scribe can Him describe with pen,
He's fairer than the sons of men.
The loving labors of His hands
The starry sky by far outspans.

All lesser glories fade and wane,
The treasures of His love remain,
The pleasures of His peace abide,
For light and life in Him reside.

For Christ is chief in constancy
And lowliest in humility;
His love shines forth in golden ray
To brighten all the homeward way.

From His fair face we fully trace
The secret source of every grace;
The greatest glory of His fame
Is centered in His precious Name.

I am Alpha and Omega (Rev. 22:13).

Explorers who have ventured through virgin forests covering mountainous country never before penetrated by man have betimes reached a vantage point whence they caught a glimpse of a gorgeous valley of unsuspected splendor. The sight of stately trees with their masses of foliage draping the slopes is suddenly enhanced by virtue of the eyes alighting on a fairylike waterfall, set in rich emerald surroundings at the head of the gorge. The new discovery lends charm and character to the whole landscape.

Much more than the picturesque waters add to the scenic beauties of nature's magnificence, Christ supplies in the spiritual sphere celestial verities to all aspects of sacred virtue. He lends charm to contentment, beauty to beneficence, mercy to might, sympathy to strength, amiability to authority, meekness to majesty, glory to goodness and the pleasure of permanent peace to paradise.

After traversing the broad continent of revealed truth which spreads out before us in the great panorama of the Holy Scriptures, we arrive at the journey's end in Revelation, chapter twenty-two, and there the Master Himself crowns the whole experience of our investigation by submitting one final stupendous claim. The unusual utterance Christ makes includes and incorporates every high light associated with the greatest discoveries we have made throughout the entire range of our research. Let us listen again most carefully to our Lord's culminating claim, "Behold, I come quickly; and My reward is with Me, to give every man according as his work shall be. I am Alpha and Omega, the beginning and the end, the first and the last" (Rev. 22:12-13).

Herein Christ states that the maximum of mystery is of Himself, who is the Revealer of the innermost of divine revelation. Also the mightiest witness of majesty is through Him the Creator of creation to the uttermost; and by the very nature of the munificence of mercy, we are directed to Him who is the Mediator of all mediation. "Of Him, through Him, and to Him, are all things" (Rom. 11:36). This is true from start to finish in all revelation, from commencement to consummation in all creation and from first to last in all mediation. The more we examine these words and weigh the meaning of this paramount claim of our Lord and Saviour, the more amazing and astounding they become in depth, breadth and height.

The purpose Christ had in view when making this superlative statement of claim was doubtless to remind us that behind the visible expression of His ministry, during the manifestation, lay inscrutable mysteries. Standing at the back of His mighty work in this material creation were infinite potentialities. Supporting and sustaining His matchless merit in mediation, imponderable prerogatives were secreted. The amplitude of capacity in wisdom and knowledge is focused in His person (Col. 2:3). The almightiness of ability in power and strength is likewise included; for in Him is vested all authority in heaven and on earth (Matt. 28:18). In addition, the abidingness of His ministry in grace and truth is in view; for He is all the fullness of Godhead bodily (John 1:16; Col. 2:9). These three lines of evidence assure us forever that His words are not an overstatement of claim, but the awe-inspiring truth of His monumental magnificence. Let us ask ourselves whether such an One is in a position to answer prayer, affirm pardon, assure provision and administer protection.

In Christ the whole purpose of God is centered, the fullness of Godhead concentrated and the glory of the eternal Father condensed. When our blessed Lord signifies that He is Alpha and Omega, suggesting the whole alphabet, He is using a figure relative to unceasing resource. Truly His own abilities are all unending, for He Himself is like a mine of inexhaustible wealth. He has a mind of incorruptible wisdom and He exercises a ministry of indestructible witness. In His celestial character every feature of beauty merges in perfect harmony, and the signs and symbols are exquisitely portrayed in a balanced unity. Although we may pile up figure upon figure, form upon form, and feature upon feature, all attempts that are made to adequately describe Him fall far short of the aim. The greenest leaves of loveliness, the richest fruits of faithfulness, the choicest charms of comeliness, the purest powers of peacefulness, the grandest gems of gracefulness, the brightest beams of blessedness and the fairest flowers of thoughtfulness combine in Him.

In His divine domain we may trace the springs of prophecy, whence flow the streams of history. He it is who spreads the tapestries of time athwart the august ages. He ever lives where beauty dwells in undefiled bliss, amid the undimmed brightness of glory. His workmanship is weighted with wondrous things from the tiniest mound of mercy to the towering Matterhorn of majesty. He smiles in the rainbow and laughs with the lightning. He testifies in the thunder as well as in the tiny whisper of the still small voice of calm. His heavens are studded with sparkling stars and His hands are firm but friendly. His heart is true and tender and His help is always timely. In His presence is fullness of joy and that is where stingless pleasure knows no fang of foe or pang of fear. The fair and fragrant flowers of His fervent fidelity bud and bloom eternally.

> O Christ divine, Thine is the greatest fame
>   That Truth's fair records have declared of old,
> The witness of Thy deeds and glorious Name
>   Soars higher as the mounting years unfold.
>
> O Christ divine, Thine is the greatest pow'r
>   That sways a scepter or displays a crown,
> Controlling ages and the present hour,
>   Increasing daily in Thy famed renown.
>
> O Christ divine, Thine is the greatest might,
>   No majesty nor strength compares with Thine.
> To banish darkness and establish light,
>   The Light, of Truth, which evermore will shine.

Our present study engages our attention with twelve of our Lord's titles beginning with the letter "F" and commences with the familiar designation, "Firstborn among many brethren."

THE FIRSTBORN

> For whom He did foreknow, He also did predestinate
> to be conformed to the image of His Son, that He might
> be the firstborn among many brethren (Rom. 8:29).

This special title is used in four dignified relationships in regard to our Lord Jesus Christ. In His originating energy He is the Firstborn of all creation (Col. 1:15). In His earthly manifestation, He is the Firstborn of the virgin (Luke 2:7). In His overcoming victory He is the Firstborn from the dead (Col. 1:18). In His outstanding precedence he is Firstborn among many brethren. In no single instance does birth refer to a beginning but always a manifestation; therefore our Lord's fourfold manifestation in this world is profoundly significant. The unparalleled dignity of His sublime person is unveiled as the Creator of the universe, the Crown of humanity, the Conqueror of death and the Chiefest in spiritual society.

In whatsoever direction we turn, Christ stands out supremely and sovereignly in His superior stability and surpassing sufficiency. He is pictured in His sacrificial shepherdhood in the *prima porta* of the capital city (Neh. 3:1). In princely pre-eminence He fills the highest station celestially (Heb. 7:26). As Creator He occupies the most prominent position of renown (Eph. 1:21). The uniqueness of His dignity and distinction is expressed in a variety of ways. He is first to be born a king (Matt. 2:2), first to ride the young colt (Luke 19:30), first to be laid in Joseph's new tomb (John 19:41), first in the new family of the conformed (Rom. 8:29) and first to enter for us within the veil (Heb. 6:20). This One is our family Representative and federal Head, who will one day fashion us like unto the body of His glory.

In Christ we meet unrivalled resplendence, for He expresses a fairer beauty, a richer dignity, a holier majesty and a brighter glory than all others. The Father designs to have the Son's beauty reflected in millions of living mirrors; He also decrees that His praise be chanted by myriads of loving voices; yea, and determines that His glory be commemorated by countless multitudes in lasting adoration. All are to be conformed to the image of the Firstborn. What a heritage it is to be honored as His brethren forever with the same kind of nature as our kingly Kinsman, with the same countenance as our comely Chieftain and with the same features as our famous Firstborn. The outlook glistens with the radiant hope of replete resemblance. Think for a moment of the high estimate the Father places upon His Son's exquisite excellence: the Father determines that the entire host of redeemed humanity be conformed to the beauty and royalty of His Son's perfection, a purpose which is graced with the high designs of love unsearchable. Christ holds the foremost place of honor as Head of the regenerate race, each member of which is fashioned like to Himself, displaying a facsimile of character and family likeness. Christ as Firstborn is freest in freedom's liberty, friendliest in friendly fidelity, fairest in fragrant purity and firmest in faithful constancy. "We know that, when He shall appear, we shall be like Him; for we shall see Him as He is." So we already possess the guarantee of glory, the perfect pledge of heaven itself through the Firstborn. The conception is wholly beyond the range of man's fondest imagination and constitutes one of the grandest transactions of eternity.

THE FORERUNNER

> Whither the forerunner is for us entered, even Jesus, made an high priest for ever after the order of Melchisedec (Heb. 6:20).

The entry of Christ, in triumphant stateliness as our Forerunner, is the greatest guarantee that could possibly be imparted that the generous gifts of salvation He gained by His cross will be graciously given to all who by faith follow on in the race set before them. We are definitely told later that He entered with His own blood (Heb. 9:12), which constitutes the factor and the means whereby He vanquished the foe and gained the victory, and by virtue of which His redeemed people are entitled to all the privileges of the heavenly sanctuary. Both flanks of the highway entrance are protected by these immutable things, namely, by God's promise and God's oath (6:18).

Eternal realities may therefore be assured, which include "eternal salvation" (5:9), "eternal redemption" (9:12), "eternal inheritance" (9:15), "the eternal spirit" (9:14), the everlasting covenant, and such like blessings. Every spiritual privilege becomes a substantiated portion by virtue of the fact that Christ in His superior sufficiency has entered for us. His sacrificial work whereby He initiated this highway of life is infinite and final (1:3). The throne of His majestic power is invincible (1:7). His heavenly priesthood is indestructible (7:24). His precious promise is immutable (6:17). His intrinsic righteousness is impregnable (1:8). His great salvation is incorruptible (7:25). His perfect covenant is irrevocable (13:20). His spiritual blessings are innumerable (12:22-24). His gracious help knows no bounds (13:6).

The Forerunner having entered is more than a figure of speech to be interpreted; it is a fact to be insisted upon and a favor to be fully enjoyed. For Christ is now established as our Intercessor in a perpetual ministry which demonstrates the eternal values of His sacrificial suffering. In the plenitude of His power He exercises a supernatural influence and is able to save to the uttermost all who come unto God by Him (Heb. 7:25). "Wherefore . . . let us run with patience the race that is set before us, looking unto Jesus" (Heb. 12:1,2). His very countenance is a tonic to inspire, His joy is a cordial to invigorate, His promises are a stimulus to hearten and His Word is a veritable liniment of incentive to induce us to press on toward the mark for the prize of the high calling of God. What a precious basket of coronets He pledges to distribute to overcomers under the symbols of a crown of righteousness (II Tim. 4:8), a crown of life (Rev. 2:10) and a crown of glory (I Pet. 5:4).

Our Lord taught the necessity of suffering before entering into glory (Luke 24:26); crucifixion preceded coronation. "Hereunto were ye called: because Christ also suffered for us, leaving us an example, that ye should follow his steps" (I Pet. 2:21); and, "If we suffer, we shall also reign with him"

(II Tim. 2:12). How zealously we should seek to attain the zenith of approval and award and never allow flame or frown to frighten us from the shores of this everlasting inheritance. The feet of our Forerunner never falter, and we are enjoined to follow His steps. In view of our being the objects of His supreme interest and the subjects of His supernatural care, He empowers us to continue perseveringly in the things that accompany salvation. The athletes in this race are unutterably precious to Christ as they run with patience the onward, upward, heavenward way, enamored of their lovely Leader, who enables them to sing in the roughest ways, serve in the darkest days and surmount the surging waves by virtue of their looking unto Him.

Love is the divinest reality in the revelation of Christ, who Himself reconciles us in righteousness and renews us in resemblance to His own likeness. He has entered, in order to prepare a palatial home of glory for His people in a paradise of pleasure. There His people will be environed by the supreme delights of joy, enraptured by the music of His name, entranced by the sweetness of His love, engraced by His perfect image.

THE FIRSTFRUITS

But now is Christ risen from the dead, and become the firstfruits of them that slept (I Cor. 15:20).

"How amiable are Thy tabernacles, O Lord of hosts!" Such an expression of delight might well be used of those joyous courts within the precincts of which the annual commemorations of the enlightening and enriching ceremonies of seven great national feasts were celebrated. These feasts, of which the firstfruits is but one, not only furnished the nation of Israel with continual enlightenment in relation to God's dealings under local conditions, but also forecast the future course of national experience until Messiah was manifested, through whose mission and ministry the true significance of the symbolism would reach final fruition. As an example of New Testament fulfillment we find it expressly declared in the most explicit words that Christ is our Passover and the First-fruits (I Cor. 5:7; 15:20). How plainly and potently the whole of these ceremonial ordinances direct us to One who is the competent Redeemer, the consummate Deliverer, the consistent Saviour and the complete Sustainer. He establishes the eternal realities reflected in the symbolism of Israel's seven national feasts.

The redemptive calendar of the nation began with the commemoration of the Passover. The Passover had the purpose of recalling the Lord's deliverance from Egyptian bondage. During the seventh month the Feast of Tabernacles completed the series. Three of these seven were compulsory for all the inhabitants of the land from twenty years old and upward. (Our Lord in His ministry illustrated in a matchless manner these three in Luke 15. The figures He used were those of a shepherd and the lost sheep, a searcher and the lost silver and a sire and his lost son.) The festivals were marked with great rejoicing and the range of celebration covered the entire experience and expectation of the nation historically, ceremonially and prophetically.

Vital lessons may be traced from following the order in which the sacred seasons were ordained. The Feast of Passover expressed redemption; Christ is the Redeemer. The Feast of Firstfruits emphasized resurrection; Christ is the Resurrection and the Life. The Feast of Weeks (later called Pentecost) signified regeneration; Christ is the Regenerator. The Feast of Atonement demonstrated reconciliation; Christ is the Reconciler. The Feast of Trumpets proclaimed release and repossession; Christ is the Ransomer. The Feast of Tabernacles exhibited re-creation; Christ is the Re-creator, who makes all things new. The Feast of Sabbath assured divine repose; Christ is the replete Rest.

Each one of the seven presents Christ in an outstanding feature of His person and work. The fulfillment of the first three was necessary for the establishment of the Church. The utmost of the spiritual values reflected in these feasts was realized in Christ, the true substance who completed the full significance of all that they typified according to the appointed dates specified in the Jewish calendar. The next three require fulfillment for the manifestation of the kingdom. In their setting of old they were confined as to date and design to within the radius of one month. Attention is drawn to the consummation of these latter three feasts in the book of the Revelation, chapters seven, eleven and nineteen. Beyond these the sabbath that remaineth for the people of God will be entered as an everlasting rest.

In these picturesque festivals, which reflected past history, required reasonable habits and reassured anticipated hopes, the complete prophetic panorama of God's dealings is visualized and outlined. In them can be traced the course of the centuries from the time of the first Passover celebrated in Egypt to that final homecoming depicted in the Feast of Tabernacles, when the ransomed of the Lord shall return and come with everlasting joy upon their heads and sorrow and sighing shall flee away (Isa. 35:10).

This prophetical portrayal of the eternal purpose comprises one of the most magnificent forecasts to be found anywhere in Scripture, and is utterly beyond the capability of the human mind to have originated. The Apostle Peter reminds us that we have a more sure word of prophecy unto which we do well to take heed; for in the instance of Christ, the witness comes from "the excellent glory," from God Himself directly and absolutely substantiates that the fulfillment of all final things is through Christ (II Pet. 1:17-19).

If Christ be not the Firstfruits, then the whole fabric of the Jewish economy is meaningless and the entire formula of the Christian faith valueless. Morever, the extensive system of symbolic representation coloring the Scriptures would become aimless and profitless. We are not relying on fables for our confidence. The resurrection of Christ as the Firstfruits guarantees, with all certitude, that the redeemed of the Lord shall also be raised. Christ is the vital and veritable demonstration that death is to be destroyed (I Cor. 15:54), and His vanquishing power stands as an imperishable monument to the immortal majesty and the prevailing victory of His glorious might.

Christ has added a new emphasis to every syllable of the national history of Israel as reflected in these feasts and has illumined them with the eternal light of spiritual reality. How very necessary it was that an incorruptible Champion should arise to challenge and conquer the foe of faith and friendship, and establish the cause of freedom and fellowship forever.

Many of the philosophers of Greece considered revelation from God as something mythical; wherefore the Apostle Paul, in his message to the Corinthians of that country, verifies that Christ is the true Passover (I Cor. 5:7); Christ is the real Firstfruits (15:20); and Christ is the sure Rock (10:4), from which flowed the stream of spiritual supply by which Jew and Gentile were baptized as living members into the body of Christ (12:12-13).

We might well say, O glorious Christ of infinite merit, that Thine own unrivalled majesty entitles Thee to represent us in all relationships of Firstborn, Forerunner and Firstfruits, not merely with a distinction that glorifies God, but with a benefaction toward man which transforms and transfigures into Thine own likeness. When we see Thee, the Firstfruits, we shall be like Thee. To Thee our thanks, our praise, our love. Amen.

THE FAITHFUL ONE

> And unto the angel of the church of the Laodiceans write: These things saith the Amen, the faithful and true witness, the beginning of the creation of God (Rev. 3:14).

The book of Revelation, above all others, directs our faith to the one grand center of attraction in the celestial system, where the pre-eminence of Christ is particularly revealed. The marvelously unfolded spectacle of His virtuous excellency enraptures all heaven and awakens reverent homage and rapturous praise from countless multitudes. Among the many manifestations given of His manifold offices, we are permitted to view Him in His marvelous sovereignty as Saviour, the Son of man; in His spacious glory as Creator, for whom are all things; in His wondrous regency as Redeemer, alone worthy to take the title deeds; in His gracious constancy as Shepherd, leading by fountains of living waters; in His prodigious ministry as Mediator, with one foot on land and one on the sea; in His victorious dignity as Deliverer, beside the crystal sea; in His glorious majesty as King of kings, crowned with many diadems; in His stupendous authority as Lord of lords, marshalling His heavenly hosts for war; in His righteous integrity as Judge of all, seated upon the great white throne; and in His lustrous beauty as Bridegroom, adorning the greatest marriage celebrations ever witnessed.

All of these wondrous vocations are associated and identified with His sacrificial character as the Lamb.

Christ is the personification of reality, verity and integrity. The words He spoke when on earth have not diminished in their authority and authenticity one iota. No one else exists whose words abide the centuries in vigor and vitality, in freshness and faithfulness. The witness of One who is faithful and true never wears away with the waning of the years, nor dies down with the decay of worldly dominions. The imperishable charge Christ gave as a challenge to His Church two thousand years ago is as changeless as His own character: "He that hath ears to hear let him hear." "Behold, I stand at the door, and knock: if any man hear My voice, and open the door, I will come in to him, and will sup with him, and he with Me" (Rev. 3:20).

In His faithful witness our Lord did not trifle over transient things, but testified to eternal Truth. He never pandered to the populace to gain popularity or praise. He never minimized nor falsified any reality, nor groped and guessed at any time when giving an answer to a question. No taunt or trifle marred the trend of His thoughtful tenderness. No blame or blemish blurred the brightness of His stainless beauty. No sear or scar stemmed the sensitive flow of His strong sympathy. No flaw or fickleness blighted the fervor of His faithful fidelity to truth and love.

> Bring forth the royal diadem
> And crown Him Lord of all.

In His message to mankind He unveiled the mysteries of God, revealed the treasure of truth, foretold the future of nations and disclosed the issues of life. His testimony to things unseen is too profound for even the greatest philosophers to fully explain or expound. The illustrations He used were of the most familiar kind such as catching fish, buying foot, patching garments, seeking treasure, losing money, finding sheep, giving alms and scores of other common everyday happenings. When He made use of historic announcements of a prophetic nature, He spake as a prophet mighty in word and matchless in wisdom. Nothing He said ever needed to be recalled, nothing He taught ever required correction and He never had to apologize for a misguided statement. He spake with an unparalleled and perfect excellence of expression, with an unprecedented spiritual intelligence and insight and with an unrivalled and eminent eloquence, unshackled by a limited learning. No battle-axe or buckler can resist His sayings and no shield of steel can stem the irresistible sword thrust of His Spirit from reaching the conscience. His lips are likened in Scripture to lovely lilies (S. of Sol. 5:13), while the remarks He made on the flowers of the field are as redolent as the rose buds themselves.

The witness He bore to visible and invisible alike was worthy of His incarnate Deity. The words He used when condemning or commending were wisely chosen. The woes He uttered against wickedness and hypocrisy were intended to warn those who have ears to hear to flee from the wrath to come. His testimony to judgment and justification, to creation and consummation, to redemption and regeneration, to the Father's purpose and the future prospects were wholly faithful and true.

> He never sold the truth to serve the hour,
> Nor bartered with the world in seeking power.
> He let the sullen stream of rumor flow
> And pandered not to hearers high or low.
> His life consumed with zeal and ardent toil,
> He spake in loving words, heaven-hewn and royal.

THE FOUNTAIN OF LIFE

For with Thee is the fountain of life: in Thy light shall
we see light (Ps. 36:9).

Seven significant suggestions are given in the immediate
context of this Psalm to portray the familiar characteristics of
the life that ever flows from this Fountain. The very form of
these divine demonstrations unveils the beauty of the inner
character of that holy life which is so full-orbed. Let us
recount the manifold qualities which are so dramatically
expressed. His lovingkindness, which is rendered "mercy," is
heavenly in its magnificence and magnitude (v. 5). His
faithfulness is witnessed in the wonderful clouds that refresh
the earth (v. 5). His judgments are more profound than
unfathomable depths (v. 6). His righteousness is as majestic as
the massive mountains (v. 6). His preserving care for the
protection of His creatures is without partiality (v. 6). His
exceptional excellence excels in beneficence and provides the
sheltering comfort of sympathetic wings for consolation (v.7).

Christ is the source and supply, yea, the very spring of all
such attributes of life. Every figure that is used in Scripture to
express Him in any of His capacities is the most forceful
illustration of fullness conceivable. The flow of this Fountain
never diminishes, for Christ is ceaselessly distributing fresh
vitality to energize His people for enthusiastic endeavor. He is
ever divulging fresh secrets in vision and dream to enlighten
the mind with greater comprehension. He is ever displaying
fresh virtues to endear Himself to the heart's affection. He is
ever disclosing fresh verities to enrich our knowledge of the
Father. He is ever deciding fresh visits to enliven the spirit into
deeper participation and fellowship. Yea, and He is ever
determining fresh victories to encourage His servants in
aggressive ministry.

Every feature of vigor and virtue in the life of faith flows
from this Fountain. Whether it be the life of loyalty in
devotion expressed in Abraham, the life of dignity in the
ability of Moses, the life of majesty in the royalty of David, the

life of purity in the sincerity of Daniel, the life of constancy in the fidelity of Ezra, the life of generosity in the liberality of Nehemiah, or the life of sympathy in the brotherly love of Barnabas; the totality of manifold excellence emanates from Him.

> Oh, Christ! He is the Fountain,
>   The deep sweet Well of love;
> The streams on earth I've tasted,
>   More deep I'll drink above;
> There to an ocean fullness
>   His mercy doth expand,
> And glory, glory dwelleth
>   In Emmanuel's land.

THE FOUNDATION

For other foundation can no man lay than that is laid, which is Jesus Christ (I Cor. 3:11).

The Apostle Paul assures us in chapter two of this Epistle that he preached but one subject (2:2), he affirms that he presented one foundation (3:11), he asserts that the plan of God provides for one body (12:12) and avows that the entire purpose is being promoted by one Spirit (12:13).

We know Christ to be the surest, strongest and most steadfast Foundation that was ever laid. He cannot fail or fall, and is for the upbuilding of God's eternal purpose. One of the great essentials in the effectual construction of Christian character is a continuous and consistent witness to Christ in all His manifold sufficiency. Primarily, the whole of the divine purpose rests upon Him. Particularly, the entire program relies upon Him for its fulfillment. Pre-eminently, the perfecting of the kingdom in permanent righteousness also devolves on Him for establishment.

Christ is not only the Founder and Foundation of the Church, but also of the commonwealth, and He is the Founder and Foundation of the City of God. The benefits and blessings of all three depend solely upon Him. The same is true also of the unanimity, uniformity and unity of all divine construction. Our reconciliation depends on Him, our acceptance devolves upon Him and our association in the society of God is derived through Him. Christ is God's Foundation in relation to His will, His wisdom and His work. No realization of eternal salvation, effectual justification, or eventual glorification is possible without Him. His credentials testify to His trustworthiness; His reliable majesty and resolute authority are sure to triumph.

"Other foundation can no man lay than that is laid, which is Jesus Christ (I Cor. 3:11; II Tim. 2:19). We should seek more than a mere glimpse of the durable grandeur of our Lord's unvarying authority and learn to gaze upon the matchless glory of His constancy, integrity and fidelity, until the majestic loveliness of His personal splendor is indelibly impressed upon our minds.

> God's foundation standeth sure,
>   By Him in Zion laid,
> Which none can shake, much less remove,
>   Why should we be afraid?
> Afraid of man's philosophy,
>   His science or his doubt?
> If we have such disloyal fears
>   May God soon cast them out.

THE FAIRER THAN MEN

> Thou art fairer than the children of men: grace is poured into Thy lips: therefore God hath blessed Thee for ever (Ps. 45:2).

"Fairer," "greater," "better," "higher" and the like terms are familiar references in relation to Christ, throughout Scripture, when comparison is made of Him in relation to other notables. All other stars borrow their brilliance from the Bright and Morning Star, all other suitors borrow their beauty and charm from this beloved Bridegroom. Our Well-beloved is without blemish, fairer than the whitest wings of purest joy, fairer than the precious plumage of perfect peace, yea, fairer than the priceless perfume of redolent love.

If we pause to consider our surroundings, the whole realm of creation is studded with lustrous illustrations of fairness in the lilies, daybreaks, sunsets and such like. Further afield are the snow-clad mountain peaks, the scintillating stars and stainless sunlight, all of which reflect the unsullied beauty of material things. Yet these are but dim shadows in comparison with the highest, purest and richest excellence which radiates from the character of the Lord Jesus, whose comeliness never corrodes, whose fairness never fades, whose liveliness never languishes. The fairest flowers of the field, the most luscious fruits of the orchard and the most luxuriant gardens of every clime pale in the presence of God's well-beloved Son.

A vision of Him always verifies the verdict of revealed truth, for "He is fairer than the children of men." This is definitely sustained by the radiant regality of His righteousness, by the peerless purity of His perfectness, by the gracious generosity of His goodness, by the tranquil transparency of His truthfulness, by the stainless sincerity of His sinlessness, by the sterling sublimity of His spotlessness and by the healthsome harmony of His holiness.

Christ holds the most endearing title, Bridegroom; He has the most engrossing name, Jesus; He has the most enduring designation, the Truth; He has the most enriching office, that of High Priest; He has the most enlightening vocation, namely, to reveal the Father; He has the most encouraging mission, to redeem mankind; and He has the most enrapturing motive, to glorify God. The incomparable beauty of Christ, combined with His intrinsic purity and inconceivable glory, confirms that He is the Fairer than Men.

We are highly favored to have such an estate of riches wherein our hearts' affection may revel, and such an inheritance of righteousness in which our minds may roam, and such a habitation of rest where our souls may rejoice, as His own blessed person. How much we need an eye sanctified by the Spirit to really behold Him in His fairness.

THE FRIEND OF SINNERS

The Son of man is come eating and drinking; and ye
say, Behold a gluttonous man, and a winebibber, a friend
of publicans and sinners! (Luke 7:34)

The true essence of friendship is expressed by love's highest
esteem. Wherever such flourishes, favors are shown, courtesies
are extended and mutual aid is given irrespective of circumstances. Therefore, a real friend is as fragrant as the
flowers, as sweet as luscious fruits and as choice as gladdening
springtide or gathered harvest. A true friend is sincere and
steadfast and is not swayed in fidelity by changing conditions.
Furthermore, the strength of such a relationship is not
sustained by fatlings from the flock or firstfruits from the
farm, so that if the flow of these things should fail all
fellowship ceases. The fidelity of genuine friendship is built
with sturdier fabrics and is fixed like a firm rock which resists
the floods of adversity and flourishes when the fierce storms
rage.

The Friend referred to so frequently in Luke's Gospel is the
One who found man in the prison house and secured his
freedom by the sacrifice of Himself. When we were lost and
lone this same One "loved us, and washed us from our sins by
His own blood" (Rev. 1:5). The infinite heart of this eternal
Friend loves us with an everlasting love. The fadeless laurels of
abiding friendship befit no other brow but His. He has the
power to blind us with a sudden flash of His brilliant glory, or
banish us with a single behest into the blackness of darkness.
Instead, He befriends and assures us acceptance in Himself,
the Beloved (Eph. 1:6). "What a friend we have in Jesus, all
our sins and griefs to bear."

This faithful Friend has pledged never to leave or forsake us
(Heb. 13:5); though we be changeful, He changes not; His
constancy never diminishes; He firmly adheres to His purpose.
He will perfect us and present us before the presence of His
glory with exceeding joy. He has prepared supernal splendors
for those who trust in Him before the sons of men (I Cor. 2:9).
The heart of this Friend is a veritable spring of sympathy, a

fountain of favor, a citadel of compassion, a canyon of comfort, a mansion of mercy and a whole lake of lovingkindness. Christ in His friendliness is the embodiment of unselfish interest, mutual understanding and unvarying integrity. His very name radiates reality and His holy nature signifies perfect sincerity.

He is most real in friendship and entirely devoid of mere poses and pretences. His unartificial interest in mankind, beside being revealed in the Scriptures, is also reflected in the stream of time and recognized on the stage of history. His faithful integrity outshines the sun, His fervent love outlasts the stars and His friendly devotion outlives the ages. How stately and lofty are the notable characteristics of our Lord's enduring friendship, by virtue of which He has forever endeared Himself to His grateful people in an unvariable degree of constancy. The Christ, who in His might flings the golden sunrays across the horizon to gladden the heart of mankind and spreads the spacious sky of azure to form a background for myriad scintillating stars, is untiring in his vigilant watchfulness. Although loftiest in honor, He is lowly in heart and observant of the least and loneliest, and considerate of the poorest and plainest of men. He is the "Friend that loveth at all times."

THE FELLOW OF GOD

> Awake, O sword, against My shepherd, and against the man that is My fellow, saith the LORD of hosts: smite the shepherd, and the sheep shall be scattered: and I will turn Mine hand upon the little ones (Zech. 13:7).

This relationship cites a mutual companionship amicable in its association and co-operative in an activity where perfect accord reigns supreme. The moral glories of Christ which qualify Him to be an Associate of God are absolutely unmarred and unblemished. He is wholly suited for intimacy and identity with the Father of lights in mind and will and purpose. Christ never defiled or debased His affections, He never assumed or asserted self-will in the slightest degree and He never amended or assailed the Word of God in motive or meditation. Here we discover complete likeness expressed in unity, amity and harmony, which in turn are demonstrated in close association, concerted action and complete administration. During the manifestation, Christ not only revealed and resembled the Father but represented Him in every detail and could say without hesitation, "He that hath seen Me hath seen the Father" (John 14:9). His countenance reflected the glory of the Father (John 1:14), His compassion expressed the grace of the Father (John 5:19, 20) and His competence displayed the greatness of the Father (John 10:27).

This same Fellow of God, who became the sinless substitute for man, was also smitten of God, as disclosed in the words, "Smite the shepherd and the sheep shall be scattered." (Our Lord quoted this statement before He drank the dread cup in Gethsemane.) The blessed Saviour did not find His supreme pleasure by claiming His inherent rights of equality with God, but sought an honor that was obtainable only by voluntary sacrifice in a self-abnegating service (Phil. 2:7-8). He reveled not in His own rightful glory but resolved to redeem and regenerate man and to bestow glory on the sons of men. In so doing He has secured and added a new glory to the crown of Deity. A great host that no man can number will be glorified with Him. "Wherefore God also hath highly exalted Him, and given Him a name which is above every name" (v. 9). We have now been made "fellow-citizens with the saints, and of the household of God" (Eph. 2:19), to the wonder and admiration of myriads of angels. In the eternal vigor of His own immortal virtue He assures to His people unending relationship and ratifies the imperishable bond of His everlasting fellowship.

THE FIRST

I was in The Spirit on the Lord's day, and heard
behind me a great voice as of a trumpet saying, I am
Alpha and Omega, The first and the last (Rev. 1:10-11).

The final unveiling is given in order to fully identify the

deity of Christ, and is therefore most dramatic in its movements, most prophetic in its magnificence and most historic in its message. Reigning at the very summit of superiority, subjugating all things to Himself and sustaining the freeborn hosts of mankind is the Lamb in the midst of the throne.

Yet, withal, these final consummations could never have matured had there not been a beginning. Standing on the threshold of primal creation is Christ the first and foremost. The designation is singularly sovereign in its sublime grandeur and indicates the precedence of One who is supremely superior in wisdom and solitarily sufficient in will and purpose to initiate the entire plan of creation, redemption and mediation.

By virtue of this timeless and ageless title, the First, Christ is wholly independent in intellectual sensibility, volitional stability and emotional sympathy. Behind the transient ministry of the manifestation, when the divine mind, will and heart were expressed, lies a transcendent mystery. Christ, the First, eternally possessed the credentials of everlasting readiness, resourcefulness and resoluteness to redeem. His qualifications assure an age-abiding ability and aptitude to make reconciliation and maintain its meritorious ad-ministration. His eternal excellence enables Him efficiently and efficaciously to effect the erasure of all transgression, to emancipate man from the thraldom of sin and to establish righteousness for evermore. The verities of His inherent virtue were evident when He voluntarily became Son of man and by His vicarious sufferings and victorious resurrection demon-strated the glories of the invisible God.

Our Lord's claim, "I am the First," is a revelation of His almighty authority, His essential energy and His inherent infinity, all of which are aglow at the beginning with moral glory and spiritual sublimity. Yea, He means by this declaration that He is the independent "I AM," the Originator of creative counsels and the Ordainer of primal powers.

The One who is everlastingly effulgent as the light, and the everliving Lord of love, is Himself the well-spring of wisdom, the fountain of faithfulness and the reservoir of revelation. Christ, the First, is therefore the sole source of spiritual strength, the repository of righteousness and the habitation of holiness. Without controversy He is the First in expressing the fullness of the Godhead, the First as the Father's resemblance, the First as the Framer of creation, the First as the Fountain of life, the First as the Founder of faith, the First as the Forgiver of sins, the First as the Fellow of God, the First as the Faithful Witness, the First as a faultless sacrifice, the First in His mastery over death and in scores of other offices and vocations, everyone of which contributes to the glory of His supernatural name and to His divine nature.

THE FULLNESS OF GODHEAD

> For it pleased the Father that in Him should all fulness dwell (Col. 1:19).
> For in Him dwelleth all the fulness of the Godhead bodily (2:9).

This is one of the most stupendous of the sensational statements made in the New Testament concerning the greatness of our Lord Jesus Christ. The designs of Deity complacently determined that in Him should all fullness dwell to a degree and a dimension wholly undefinable by humanity, because of the vastness involved. The investiture of Christ with such fullness magnifies His all-sufficiency insuperably. The idea of the word inculcates infinity, includes versatility and incorporates finality. Herein is combined everything of supreme strength, replete resource, absolute authority and complete competence. Concerning Christ it may be stated that by virtue of this sanction He is the fullness of every celestial attribute, the citadel of every spiritual verity, the center of every moral glory and the custodian innermost of everything vital and the uppermost of all that is vocational. What measureless fullness Christ Himself incorporated of life and light, love and law, power and purpose, majesty and mastery, supremacy and sufficiency, merit and mercy, grace and glory! Unspeakable consolation should result from our knowing that the infinite and interminable riches of wisdom and treasures of knowledge, which dwell in Christ our Redeemer, are assured forever; for He can never be deposed by a superior, nor be displaced by a successor, nor defeated by a stronger. His status of pre-eminence is never in jeopardy.

Every conceivable capability is centered in Him completely, and every effulgent excellence is enshrined in His character entirely. Maybe the simplest way to express this fullness in all its profusion would be to say that in Christ we meet the fullness of creative power, the fullness of redeeming love, the fullness of revealing light, the fullness of enduring life, the fullness of mediating mercy, the fullness of perfecting grace and the fullness of everlasting glory. These manifold glories of Christ are reflected in His sovereign rights, superior resources, supreme relationships and superlative reasons which operate for carrying into effect God's eternal purpose. This notable Redeemer is Lord of Life, Heir of all things, Head of every man, and Chief among ten thousand.

When we consider the winsomeness of His personal beauty, the handsomeness of His potential superiority and the awesomeness of His perennial glory, our highest conceptions of His splendor are imperfect, our loudest anthems of praise in His honor are inadequate, our choicest descriptions of His demeanor are insipid and our greatest interpretations of His grandeur are insignificant.

In the light of this exhaustless fullness which dwells in Christ, who is the only One qualified to contain such infinities, each one of us is responsible to ensure that our vessel is filled full in Him and renewed and replenished daily (Col. 2:9-10).

THE FORGIVER OF SINS

> And when He saw their faith, He said unto him, Man, thy sins are forgiven thee . . . . Who can forgive sins, but God alone? . . . But that ye may know that the Son of man hath power on earth to forgive sins . . . I say unto thee, Arise (Luke 5:20-24).

Here we meet with one of the superlative glories from the

treasury of Christ's unsearchable riches. The precious act of forgiving sins is one of the highest of the princely prerogatives associated with the priestly administration of the Son of man. Paul places this gracious ministry among the "all spiritual blessings" referred to in Ephesians 1:3, in which section it is listed with those massive truths of greatest stature such as election, predestination and adoption. The profound doctrines of an ageless past would be of little worth to us apart from an actual experience of the present to be richly enjoyed. "In whom we *have* redemption through His blood, the forgiveness of sins, according to the riches of His grace" (Eph. 1:7).

When our Lord notified the paralytic that his sins were forgiven him, the reasoning Pharisees, who failed to perceive in Christ the Emmanuel, immediately questioned the Master's divine authority by saying, "Who can forgive sins, but God alone?" The bestowal of forgiveness is the favor of an infinite faithfulness, by virtue of Christ's having furnished in full the payment sought by the righteous requirements of celestial justice against the guilt of sin. What is more amiable and appealing in the handsome dignity of almighty love than the divine disposition to forgive? The sanction is a sequel to the redeeming sacrifice of the Son of man, "who through the eternal Spirit offered Himself without spot to God" (Heb. 9:14). Heaven's high throne has been honorably upheld, holiness has been glorified and mercy magnified most creditably with everlasting distinction.

Do we really honor the Lord Jesus by fully believing that He freely and frankly forgives? Let us not dishonor His dignity by doubting Him. One of the greatest griefs Joseph encountered in his outstanding career came shortly after his father's death. A deputation from among his own brethren who had so grievously wronged him in earlier life approached his lordship to ascertain if he were contemplating retaliation for their misdeeds, in view of their father Jacob having died (Gen. 50:17-18). Joseph wept with grief to think that his brethren doubted the genuineness of his wholehearted forgiveness.

Let us come to Him unafraid, remembering that He said,

"Him that cometh to Me I will in no wise cast out" (John 6:37). When Peter met John Mark after his lapse through lack of courage and sought to restore him, Peter was able to tell the discouraged disciple how in an hour of challenge he himself had denied his Lord with oaths and curses, but was reassured of forgiveness and graciously recommissioned.

Throughout his long life of service the Apostle Paul never lost the sense of wonderment and worship at the thought of his own forgiveness. He said to Timothy toward the close of his career that he was before a blasphemer, a persecutor and injurious, but now had obtained mercy and been put in trust with this ministry. To be both forgiven and trusted by such a Master as Christ caused Paul to marvel greatly, and these were experiences which formed in him a forgiving spirit (II Cor. 2:10).

If we deeply reverence the medium of divine manifestation in the Son of man, if we duly recognize the magnitude of divine mercy in the sufficiency of His grace and definitely realize the majesty of divine mediation in the suffering and supplication of the Saviour, we will not doubt the reality of the kindness of God in Christ Jesus' demonstrating the beneficent act of forgiveness. This attitude of infinite holiness in showing such clemency rests on the righteous basis of a sevenfold plea which may be stated briefly as follows:

The plea of the saviourhood of Christ, Matt. 9:6: "That ye may know that the Son of man hath power on earth to forgive sins."

The plea of the sacrifice of Christ, Eph. 1:7; also Col. 1:14: "In whom we have redemption through His blood, the forgiveness of sins."

The plea of the sympathy of Christ, Luke 7:42: "And when they had nothing to pay he frankly forgave them both."

The plea of the sufficiency of Christ, Mark 2:5-7: "When Jesus saw their faith, He said . . . Son, thy sins be forgiven thee . . . . Who can forgive sins but God only?"

The plea of the sonship of Christ, Luke 23:34: "Then said Jesus, Father, forgive them; for they know not what they do."

The plea of the substitution of Christ, I John 1:9: "If we

confess our sins, He is faithful and just to forgive us our sins, and to cleanse us from all unrighteousness."

The plea of the supplication of Christ, Heb. 7:25: "He is able to save them to the uttermost . . . seeing He ever liveth to make intercession for them."

"If thou, Lord, shouldest mark iniquities, O Lord, who shall stand? But there is forgiveness with Thee, that Thou mayest be feared" (Ps. 130:3-4). Forgiveness is one of the noblest splendors of God's abounding grace, one of the richest grandeurs of Christ's abiding mercy and one of the choicest demeanors of the Spirit's abundant love.

G

The immutability of God the Father, the infallibility of the Spirit of Truth, and the incorruptibility of Holy Scripture witness to the distinctive qualities of the Redeemer.

The GLORY OF GOD (John 1:14)
> He is the effulgence of ineffable light.

The GIFT OF GOD (John 4:10)
> He is the lustrous legacy from heaven.

The GOOD MASTER (Matt. 19:16)
> Christ the subsistence of God's character.

The GREAT HIGH PRIEST (Heb. 4:14)
> Our suitability for access and acceptance.

The GREATER THAN SOLOMON (Matt. 12:42)
> Wholly superior in sovereign majesty.

The GREATER THAN JONAH (Matt. 12:41)
> Christ surpasses all in perfect submission.

The GREATER THAN JACOB (John 4:12)
> Able to transfigure the soul and transform the life.

The GAZELLE (Prov. 30:31)
> His effective endeavor to emancipate.

The GUIDE EVEN TO DEATH (Ps. 48:14)
> His wise counsel and wondrous care.

The GOVERNOR AMONG NATIONS (Ps. 22:28)
> Infinite in His imperial independence.

The GATHERER OF LAMBS (Isa. 40:11)
> The gentleness of almighty greatness.

The GLORIOUS LORD (Exod. 15:11, Isa. 33:21)
> The exclusive attribute of His Deity.

THE IMAGE OF THE INVISIBLE GOD

CHRIST IS THE REPLICA OF DIVINE REALITY

> *He reflected the light of Life*
> *He resembled the glory of God*
> *He radiated the title of Truth*
> *He released the gifts of Grace*
> *He revealed the love of God*
> *He realized the peace of Purity*
> *He received the honor of Heaven*

HE IS ALTOGETHER LOVELY

Oh Christ! there is no deeper joy than Thine,
   Anointed highest in the realm of bliss;
Thy many diadems a worthy sign
   As signal tokens of Thy righteousness.

Oh Christ! there is no wider power than Thine,
   Superior in omnipotence and might;
A Messenger of mercy to refine,
   Thou perfect Son, the Father's chief delight.

Oh Christ! there is no richer grace than Thine,
   No peer nor equal ranks along with Thee;
The fullness of Thy treasures far outshine,
   For grace and truth embellish sanctity.

Oh Christ! there is no brighter face than Thine,
   The matchless features of a perfect form;
Thy love-lit eye beyond compare so fine
   Reflects Heav'n's perfect beauty at its norm.

Oh, Christ! there is no calmer peace than Thine,
   By angels heralded one holy morn,
So deep and real, a quietness divine,
   Like silent sunbeams in the noiseless dawn.

Oh Name of ceaseless music, endless song,
   Above all names and claims in boundless praise,
The priceless treasure of a countless throng
   Which magnifies Thy love in joyful lays.

I am Alpha and Omega (Rev. 22:13).

Wherever we contemplate our Lord in His manifold labors, the luster of His lovingkindness is never lacking, the burnish of His beauty is never dull, the resplendence of His radiance is never pale, the vigor of His vitality is never faint, the state of His strength is never stale, the wisdom of His will is never warped and the faithfulness of His fidelity never falters. Therefore, the prospect of His perfecting His Church according to His eternal purpose can never perish.

We are dealing with realities that are steadfast forevermore, inasmuch as standing behind the person of this indispensable and indestructible Christ we discover the immutability of God the Father, the infallibility of the Spirit of truth and the incorruptibility of Holy Scripture. In the light of such things we require a capable witness, qualified with celestial credentials to set forth the distinctive qualities of the Redeemer of mankind. Who then is better suited to do this than the Lord Himself? For no human agent knows who the Son is, nor can he portray the capacities and capabilities of such a celebrity (Luke 10:22). Let us revere His testimony and review again and again the magnitude of His magnificent claim, "He that sat upon the throne said, Behold I make all things new. And He said to me, Write: for these words are true and faithful. And He said unto me, It is done. I am Alpha and Omega, the beginning and the end. I will give unto him that is athirst of the fountain of the water of life freely" (Rev. 21:5, 6).

What a portrayal this is of our Lord's divine potentiality! His words are unsurpassed as a royal announcement and unparalleled in regal achievement. No declaration ever made by any national leader the world over throughout the historic ages is comparable to this statement uttered by the risen Christ. From the uppermost realm of His supreme power He announces the uttermost decree of His sublime purpose, and charges that it shall be written in black and white as a living, lasting record. Herein, by a glorious declaration, He crystallizes that which He visualizes when addressing His disciples (Matt. 19:28). His supreme declaration, "Behold I make all things new," leads to a special charge, "Write: for these words are true and faithful." Then follows a steadfast assurance "It is done," supported by His sublime claim, "I am Alpha and Omega, the beginning and the end"; and all this is accompanied by His splendid offer, "I will give unto him that is athirst of the fountain of the water of life freely." His words stand the test of time and abide the assizes of the ages.

Whenever we turn on earth to contemplate men of ability and dignity, we cannot help observing their limitations; but in Christ we meet limitlessness. Likewise the authority of all who wield administrative powers is marked by boundaries, but in Him we find One who is boundless. If we turn to consider the capability of those in national leadership, every one is circumscribed by the contingencies of the hour and by the confines of time; but the Lord Jesus is timeless. Even though the resources of every other celebrity in high command can be measured by material standards, the resources of this Claimant are measureless. Furthermore, when men of renown reach the borders of maturity, old age robs them of vitality, vision and venture; but the son of God is ageless and wholly immune from mortality. Christ spans the centuries, and the accumulating ages take no toll of His everlasting strength.

We are familiar with the names of thousands of revered worthies whose records have been emblazoned on the pages of history and in the annals of national kingdoms. Each one in turn has brought honor to a household, fame to a family, splendor to a society, glory to a generation, praise to a people, renown to a race, notoriety to a nation and well-being to a world; but Christ exceeds and excels all such, for He gained glory for the Godhead and heaped honor upon heaven. He magnified the splendor of mediatorial mercy, glorified God's generous grace and beautified the bequests of blessedness. He furnished the foundations of faith and is the abiding Author of eternal salvation, the One who satisfies infinite justice and who justifies all who believe.

Messiah is never more radiant than when He reveals the resplendence of the divine mercy, the righteousness of the divine mastery and the regality of the divine majesty. He is never more precious than when He presents His celestial credentials of partnership with the Father in the prerogatives of eternal purpose and essential power (John 5:20-29). He is never more courtly than when He is commenting on His own comeliness of character and commending His infinitely inherent capabilities (Matt. 11:25-28). He is never more princely than when He recounts His own resolute righteousness and unveils to John on Patmos His own regal resources (Rev. 1:12-16).

Our objective in this chapter is to deal with twelve of our Lord's titles and offices beginning with the letter "G."

THE GLORY OF GOD

> And the Word was made flesh, and dwelt among us, (and we beheld His glory, the glory as of the only begotten of the Father), full of grace and truth (John 1:14).

> Said I not unto thee, that, if thou wouldest believe, thou shouldest see the glory of God? (John 11:40)

Glory is as difficult to define as light, because it constitutes the exclusive excellence of the divine character in its essence and entirety, and consists of all the attributes essential to Deity blended harmoniously in perfect unity. Each characteristic is of equal proportion whether it be divine goodness, graciousness, gentleness, greatness, righteousness, resoluteness, repleteness, restfulness, pureness, perfectness, peacefulness, preciousness, lovingkindness, fullness, tenderness, mercifulness, changelessness, truthfulness, meekness, holiness, blessedness, joyfulness or the score of other incorruptible qualities that comprise the very nature of Godhead. Christ in person is the exponent and full expression of every feature of Deity.

The glory of God is exhibited in the face of Jesus Christ (II Cor. 4:6). The Apostle John declares, "We beheld His glory, the glory as of the only begotten of the Father, full of grace and truth" (John 1:14). The effulgence of our Lord's beauty and dignity of character magnifies the splendor and glorifies the grandeur of all celestial perfection. The glory of

Christ is the pinnacle of the entire presentation of truth revealed in the Old Testament, the pre-eminent project of the manifestation in the New and the principal purpose set out in the final unveiling.

His glory has even greater dimensions in that the reason given for the entire creation declares that His glory should fill the whole earth (Isa. 6:3; Ps. 19:1). This fact indicates that the silvery stream, the fruitful field, the towering trees, the fragrant flowers, the verdant valleys, the prolific plains and the shimmering sea reflect His glory. The prophets likewise built the edifice of their testimony on this same foundation, and the Spirit also "testified beforehand the sufferings of Christ, and the glory that should follow" (I Pet. 1:11). The Apostle Peter makes use of "glory" sixteen times in his brief message. Glory also marked the great signs of our Saviour's ministry (John 2:11; 11:40). Yea, from the temptation, trans-figuration and triumphant ascension, all the high lights of activity demonstrate the glory of Christ. Nor are these realities and verities confined to the limits of time. The Lord has glory with the Father that was paramount before the world was (John 17:5), and this will continue to be the prevailing per-fection in the ages to come. His glory is everlasting (Eph. 3:21).

Let us not confuse this volume of witness as though it referred to material glory, the like of which is expressed in beautiful garments enriched with priceless perfume, or bountiful gardens with their prolific products of fruits and nuts that so appeal to physical senses. We are dealing with the moral glories of Christ, who is wholly independent of the trifles of luxury and trivialities of pageantry. Our Lord's bounties of grace combined with the beneficence of His goodness are spiritual blessings which issue from His own blessed character as the Beloved of the Father. Christ as Son of God reigns by moral right, and as Heir of all things rules by moral might. Therefore He is King of kings and Lord of lords. Here we find ourselves stumbling among sublimities and wandering like some lone spirit amid the spacious constellations of starry splendors.

When and where did Christ ask aid and accept acclaim from the grandeur of the sun, the brightness of the stars or the brimming fullness of the oceans? In Him dwelleth all the *fullness* of Godhead bodily, yea He is the *brightness* of God's glory (Col. 2:9; Heb. 1:3). He is not only the Lord of glory but the glory of the Lord. He is not only ageless as the Ancient of Days but abides the ages as the Altogether Lovely One. He is always awesome in beauty with the dew of His youth, amiable in ability with freshness of vigor and fairness of virtue and forever attractive in His amazing glory.

His moral characteristics apply to every feature of His fullness. He is as majestic in the glory of His meekness as in the magnificence of His might. He is the same in lowliest humility as in loftiest honor, in self-abnegating service as in supreme sovereignty; for His gentleness is born of His greatness and His integrity begotten of His immutability.

Nothing expresses the glory of God as radiantly and repletely as does the face of Jesus Christ (II Cor. 4:6). Every attribute of God in complete harmony is concentrated in Christ in exquisite beauty. When amid the acclaim of angels He ascended far above all heavens to the highest pinnacle of honor, He was adoringly admired by heavenly hosts, who never contemplate Him apart from His divine glory (for none in heaven doubts His Deity). Everything that is conceivable here falls far short of the inconceivable glory of Christ, everything comprehensible dwindles in its degree of dignity in the light of His incomprehensible greatness and goodness, and all things that are ponderable lessen in loveliness by virtue of His imponderable brightness and the brilliance of His ineffable light.

Although He is the brightness of God's glory, yet, withal, He embraces a child and encompasses a star; He expresses a whisper and employs the thunder; He tells the number of the stars and tends the broken in heart; He tints the glowing sunset with gorgeous colors for our delight and touches the leper in his grim loathsomeness to cleanse him of disease; He tunes the tones of the song birds' notes and tempers the velocity of the tornado; He transmutes clay into a sapphire and transforms a soul from corruption to celestial glory. Every whit of His work, His will and His wisdom utters His glory.

If we have no interest in this feature, there is little indication that we know Him or love Him. If we have not known the reality and rhapsody of His presence, we are not sensible of His absence when He withdraws Himself. If we have not known nearness, we shall not feel distance. We should concentrate the mind more frequently to dwell upon the glories of this invariable Lover and His investiture as Lord, until our admiration is captivated and our ravished heart revived with adoration. Our Beloved in His capacity as High Priest prayed that we might behold His glory (John 17:24). One glimpse of Him will draw out our souls to admire and direct our thoughts to desire a fuller view of His intrinsic excellence. The Apostle Paul prayed that the Ephesian Church might be blessed with this comprehension, which he said would exceed all that could be asked or thought (Eph. 3:18-20).

Such realities surpass the deformed and dying delights of this temporal world; they are the permanent perfections of durable dominion; yea, of world without end (Eph. 3:21). The Bible is the only book in man's possession that gives an account of the ages; and it depicts Christ as the center of the world to come, because He is the sole medium of expression to make known the essential glory of the invisible God.

Joseph of old desired that his father Jacob should know of all the glory he had gotten in Egypt (Gen. 45:13). When Jacob was told of it he said, "It is enough; Joseph my son is yet alive: I will go and see him before I die" (Gen. 45:28). We might well multiply our meditations on the manifold glories of so majestic a Messiah and concentrate all our faculties until we are "changed into the same image from glory to glory even as by the Spirit of the Lord" (II Cor. 3:18).

THE GIFT OF GOD

> For God so loved the world, that He gave His only begotten Son (John 3:16).

> If thou knewest the gift of God, and who it is that saith to thee, Give Me to drink; thou wouldest have asked of Him, and He would have given thee living water (John 4:10; also Rom. 6:23).

Where may we find a greater volume of profound wisdom and a deeper mine of prodigious wealth than those which God has combined in the person of His Son? What a legacy is this! The Prophet Isaiah proclaimed it centuries before in his message, "Unto us a son is given" (Isa. 9:6). In the Gift of God the infinite fullness of love, light and life reside abidingly. By virtue of this beneficent bestowment, a new comeliness has been added to the lustrousness of love, a new character to the usefulness of labor and a new charm to the sweetness of life.

Listen carefully! Seeing God hath not withheld His only Son, "How shall He not with Him also freely give us all things?" (Rom. 8:32) On the basis of the precious Gift of His infinite bounty, we are assured of everything of verity, virtue, and victory — everything of truth, treasure, and triumph; for all time. The Gift includes all spiritual excellence, all moral perfections and the uttermost of the heavenly riches of resource forevermore. The vast inheritance we have in Christ assures to us legacies that are immortal, bequests that are incorruptible and estates that are inseparable from His own personal character; for in Him we are made heirs of God. The blessed certainty of His generous guarantee burnishes the preciousness of all promise, brightens the possibilities of prayer and beautifies the pleasure of praise with more brilliant prospects (II Cor. 1:20; John 15:7; Rev. 5:9-12).

Christ, the Gift of God, outstrips all estimates. Artists cannot depict Him, poets cannot express Him, orators cannot describe Him, culture cannot appraise Him, bankers cannot value Him, earth cannot equal Him, heaven cannot match Him and angels cannot compare with Him. No scales can weigh His worth, no tables can measure His value and no standards of calculation can append a cost to *so* priceless a Gift. Included in the bestowment, we discover the fullness of His boundless grace, changeless love and fathomless mercy. Christ is God's ineffable love Gift; He is the very One who created multitudes of glistening worlds in unmeasurable space, made the priceless pearls that lie in unfathomed depths and formed the glistening gems in uncharted mines; yet, withal, He gave Himself for me!

Whoever would barter a precious diamond for a bit of dust or exchange a costly gem for a crawling worm? What hath God wrought? (Num. 23:23) "Thanks be unto God for His unspeakable gift" (II Cor. 9:15). Christ as a Gift cannot be obtained by some great performance on man's part, or merited by virtue of any human magnificence; nor is He secured by a monetary payment however great. He is a Gift to be received. "As ye have received Christ Jesus the Lord, so walk ye in Him" (Col. 2:6). "What will He not bestow, who freely gave this mighty Gift unbought, unmerited, unheeded and unsought? What will He not bestow?"

The singer and orchestra have cause to evermore combine and pour forth praises to extol the generosity of our glorious God for this crowning Gift of His openhearted love. Herein the colossal, the massive and the enormous treasures of spiritual blessings are centered in a single Gift. How can we value the invaluable or calculate the incalculable or estimate the inestimable? Since Christ has made us heirs of God, all that He is and has belongs to us: "All things are yours . . . and ye are Christ's; and Christ is God's" (I Cor. 3:21-23).

THE GOOD MASTER

And, behold, one came and said unto Him, Good Master, what good thing shall I do, that I may have eternal life? And He said to him, Why callest thou Me good? there is none good but one, that is, God (Matt. 19:16-17).

Human estimates of Christ vary considerably and the differing attitudes people hold toward Him are apparently suggested by the great variety of offerings that were permitted under the sacrificial system of the Old Testament. For instance, in the law of the sin-offering, a candidate was allowed a choice of eight different contributions ranging from a bullock down to a handful of meal. The sacrifice offered was within range of the capability and capacity of the offerer, which placed the requirement necessary for redemption within reach of all. We may divide these sanctions into three groups: the perfect, the partial and the poor. Those who brought a bullock had a perfect conception, while those who brought a dove or handful of meal had a poverty-stricken conception.

Although these values were largely determined by circumstances and the degree of enlightenment possessed, the same conditions in general pertain to the present day. According to each person's estimate of sin and need, Christ is valued and appreciated. When a person comprehends the enormity of sin and the extreme need for regeneration, appreciation of Christ's sacrifice as an offering for sin and acceptance with God will be greatly enhanced. During His manifestation, the Lord was regarded by some as merely a peasant, but by others as altogether peerless among men.

The rich young ruler recognized the inherent goodness of His character and addressed Him, "Good Master"; whereupon Christ in answering him caught up the use he made of "good," and replied, "Why callest thou Me good? there is none good but one, that is, God." The implication here is, "By your addressing Me as *Good* Master, do you really recognize that I am God?" (Read John 10:11, 33.)

Goodness is the very subsistence of God's character, and Christ is Emmanuel, God with us. A charming degree of sweetness surrounds goodness; it is not a childish trait as some suppose but is full of character and signifies a wholesomeness which savors of completeness. Christ's goodness excels in excellence and has a ring of reality infinitely above the disposition of failing mortals. The finer features of His amiable disposition and admirable nature exceed the bounds of eloquence. Goodness leads to loftier pleasures and lovelier treasures than are found here, and is always aglow with grace and glory (Ps. 84:11). Height calleth to height and depth calleth to depth. The marvels of mercy and miracles of ministry emerge from the same source. The Psalm which uses the expression, "His mercy endureth for ever" twenty-six times, commences with the words, "O give thanks unto the Lord; for He is good" (Ps. 136:1). Good is the transparent sincerity of a stainless character that acts systematically, sympathetically and sacrificially in seeking and saving the lost. All providential mercies, spiritual blessings and temporal requisites emphasize the generosity of His great goodness.

The rich ruler when he addressed Christ linked "good" with one of the seven Greek words that are rendered "master" in our English version. In this instance it is derived from *didaski*, to teach. Nicodemus so used it in John 3:2. The meaning of the title includes teaching, instructing or disciplining. The very tone and tactfulness of Christ's teaching is governed entirely by His goodness. He is in such a position and condition as to be able to make us what He is Himself. In the first chapter of Genesis, "good" is used seven times, indicating that the creative work God there wrought is a clear expression of His own character. So likewise everything Christ wrought and taught demonstrated that He is good. In His searching message found in Matthew 12:33-37, where He used "good" six times, He definitely taught that man needs regeneration in order to do good. We must first be, before we can do.

The very substance and essence of Godhead is genuine goodness, and this is the grandest characteristic of Christ's true greatness and eternal glory. Goodness has no need to conceal her identity; goodness is reasonable as well as righteous, courteous as well as cautious, confident as well as competent, providential as well as practical, patient as well as prudent, graceful as well as grateful. When goodness perceives a need, it provides for it. Goodness abhors sin and remits it. Goodness admires peace and advances it. Goodness adorns grace and assures it. Goodness approves forgiveness and advocates it. We cannot conceive of one that is better and more complete than a good person; such an one lives in a delightful state of preciousness and a charming condition of heathfulness combined with wholeness of character.

Nothing improper, impolite or imperious mars the features of Christ's good nature. He is actually the good of all goodness and the goodness of all good in expression. In Deity this means far more than possessing a virtuous quality or attribute; good is the winsome worthiness of the divine name and wholesome worshipfulness of the divine nature. Goodness constitutes the essence of Deity, the essential character that is behind every expression of grace and love, and every exhibition of the glory of light. "The LORD is good, a strong hold in the day of trouble" (Nah. 1:7); therefore good is impregnable, invincible and inestimable. Christ is all this to a degree unassignable. Because He is inherently good, He is able to make us good. He is the Sower of the good seed (Matt. 13:24); the Good Shepherd (John 10:14); and makes good (Matt. 12:33).

THE GREAT HIGH PRIEST

> Seeing then that we have a great high priest, that is passed into the heavens, Jesus the Son of God, let us hold fast our profession (Heb. 4:14).

We have a High Priest who fills the celestial throne of the heavenly sanctuary in order to maintain His people in the assurance of acceptance before the holiness of the Father. This highly exalted throne is not one of granite but of grace, not a throne of marble but of mercy, not a throne of stone but of sympathy. By virtue of the greatness of our Lord's official capacity and overseeing majesty, He has the right of relationship to redeem, the power and prerogative to save, the strength and suitability to sanctify and both the ability and affinity to ratify our acceptance for evermore. His work of maintenance as Minister of the sanctuary (Heb. 8:2) is not based upon nor born of human merit; for while we were yet without strength, "when we were enemies, we were reconciled to God by the death of his Son, much more, being reconciled, we shall be saved by his life" (Rom. 5:10).

The continual intercession of our Great High Priest at the right hand of the Majesty on high secures our salvation to the uttermost (Heb. 7:25). We possess in Christ a Priest who is in exercise of all divine rights in a state of perfect righteousness and in a ministry which is in full identity and accord with Deity, exercised on behalf of a needy humanity. For centuries past, access to the presence of kings has been considered by mortals a distinctive honor. Then what are we to think of our priceless privilege? We come into the presence of an illustrious Majesty enthroned in grace in the glory of glories, One who is the embodiment of compassionate care and who entered the eternal sanctuary for our growth in grace and for the enrichment of our spiritual sensibilities (Heb. 4:14-16). These sensibilities may be tabulated as the sense of right and wrong, which is conscience; the sense of truth and falsehood, which is reason; the sense of beauty and deformity, which is sensibility; the sense of the past, which is memory; the sense of the future, which is hope; the sense of the invisible, which is imagination; and the sense of fellowship, which is sympathy (Heb. 5:14).

In the might and merit of His majesty, Christ possesses and dispenses, by His priestly ministry, all the resources of mercy, all the requirements of mediation and all the requisites of compassion and kindness, for our maintenance before God. By virtue of this generous love, He also dispenses the riches of divine goodness, the exceeding riches of His grace and the riches of spiritual gifts which He secured on behalf of His redeemed host. His pre-eminence reflects His perfect character, which shines forth in the semblance of Godlikeness, manifesting the resplendence of the eternal glory of love. His throne is circled with a rainbow, reflecting the radiance of His exquisite beauty as the light, and His priestly work is wrought resolutely in all the rectitude of His essential authority and perfect life.

If we contemplate the glory and beauty of our Lord's priestly consecration during His earthly service, we are amazed at the degree and depth of His absolute devotion and abandonment to duty. He never deviated one iota from the path of full-orbed fidelity, not even when wreathed with thorns or while being scourged and scorned and later led out in the throes of agony to the brutal death of a baneful cross. A cruel and cursed chaplet was this, wherewith they crowned Him, the very emblem of a sin-cursed earth, which indicated far more than the betrayers intended. Christ appeared in a new role of authority that day, as King and Conqueror of that dread thing that had wrought such havoc in God's world among men; for His thorn crown signified that He was the victorious Conqueror of sin. No one but this Priest took sorrow as a scepter and thorns for a miter, as amid shame and blame He offered Himself without spot, the one perfect sacrifice for sins, and forever sat down on the right hand of God as the sign of a completed achievement. Hallelujah! What a Saviour!

Let us say in addition that His identification with humanity eclipsed everything else in the history of compassion; for He took upon Himself the form of a servant, and, "found in fashion as a man, He humbled himself, and became obedient unto death, even the death of the cross" (Phil. 2:8). By doing so He brought His own infinite resource into the enemy's domain for man's relief, the sphere in which man was held in bondage to death, so that He might defeat the Devil and deliver mankind with a strong hand and outstretched arm. Morever in undertaking this task, "He took not on Him the nature of angels; but He took on Him the seed of Abraham . . . that He might be a merciful and faithful high priest in things pertaining to God" (Heb. 2:16,17).

This praiseworthy action on Christ's part brought additional blessing, namely, the complete maintenance of our right and claims before God, which arose from the state of reconciliation secured by Christ. This aspect of His identification entailed His taking upon Himself the trouble of our transgression and acting as a substitute for our sin. "He hath made Him to be sin for us" (II Cor. 5:21). He grappled with the problem of our guilt and pollution and endured evil in responsibility on our behalf to emancipate the enthralled from the hand of the oppressor and lift us by reconciliation to share His own status of sanctity in sonship and majesty in kingship. By Him we are made kings, made heirs, made priests and made sons. What a redemption! What a reconciliation! What a regeneration!

In Christ's love there is more eloquence than in all the rhetoric of orators, and more elegance in His grace than in all the ideals of cultural organizations. No beauty of ornamentation can compare with the adornment of His spiritual perfections. His golden meekness and silvery sympathy are deftly combined with the burnished brass of His resolute courage; wherefore He is fearless in facing the foe, but friendly toward fugitives who have fled for refuge from the slayer, the dread Apollyon. In His tenderness toward us He is touched by the feeling of our infirmities; therefore we can reckon on His unfailing forbearance, His unfeigning forgiveness and His unceasing friendship. He knows, He loves, He cares. A physician must first perceive what the malady is if he would prescribe a remedy. Christ knows our need and He has the ability and sufficiency to answer for sin, assure acceptance and to adopt us into the family of God.

These things are irrefutably verified by the position He holds and the power He wields. "He is faithful that promised," and no one dare impugn the imperial integrity of His immutable Word. Let us rejoice in our access to His incorruptible throne, where we may obtain mercy and find grace to help in time of need (Heb. 4:16). One of the supreme unveilings of Christ as High Priest in the Epistle to the Hebrews shows that he precedes, succeeds and supersedes all angels and patriarchs, apostles and prophets, administrators and priests, altars and patterns, authors and pioneers, and that He abides in His preeminence as High Priest forever.

THE GREATER THAN SOLOMON

> The queen of the south shall rise in judgment with this generation, and shall condemn it; for she came from the uttermost parts of the earth to hear the wisdom of Solomon; and, behold, a greater than Solomon is here (Matt. 12:42).

The name Solomon has long since become a synonym for magnificence and majesty, wisdom and wealth, pomp and pageantry. The meaning of the title is peace, and it appears two hundred and ninety-five times on the pages of Truth. As a ruler this king became famous because of the splendor of His court, which was stamped with the impress of his far-renowned wisdom and was sustained by his remarkable wealth. His revenue in gold alone amounted to six hundred and sixty-six talents per annum, a number which marks the zenith of material grandeur.

The records of history supply a description of the character of his government, garments, grace and glory, in which things he excelled. Christ is certainly greater than Solomon in government. The scope of Solomon's jurisdiction is outlined in I Kings 4, and the boundaries of its range are specified. Christ's administration is boundless and covers heaven and earth both visible and invisible alike. During His ministry on earth, Christ clearly demonstrated His kingship in the material, physical, natural, ethical, moral, spiritual, judicial, providential and supernatural realms. His authority is definitely absolute, decidedly almighty and abiding. In all of Christ's governmental activity He demonstrates how much greater He is than Solomon.

Christ is greater than Solomon in His garments. The robes of Solomon were proverbial for beauty and attractiveness. They were made of the finest silk and beautified with the crimson-purple dye obtained from the thousands of murex shells found in profusion along the coast of Palestine. The splendor of his raiment has long since perished, but the raiment of Christ is as grand and glistening as ever. Solomon confined his adornment to His own person. When Christ drew attention to the tint and texture of the irises, lilies and purple anemones, He said, "Solomon in all his glory was not arrayed like one of these" (Matt. 6:29). But Christ might have added that in His creative work He had not limited these delightful tints and delectable textures to any one particular place or plant, but had arrayed the hills and fields of Asia, Europe, America, Africa, Australia and the islands of the seas with similar beauties. Moreover, He changes these in their manifold variety four times a year, in spring, summer, autumn, and winter. "Behold, a greater than Solomon is here." Then again Christ wore the garments of service, ministering to all. He was robed in garments of sacrifice, mediating for mankind. He was attired in the garments of salvation, in order to make sons and daughters of the living God from among the children of men. Christ imparts the spotless robe of righteousness to millions of the redeemed. "Behold, a greater than Solomon is here."

We must pass by the comparison, greater in grace, for the subject is too immense to deal with here. We go on to say a little about Christ being greater than Solomon in His glory. In our comparison we come to a point where human dignity is at its highest. However, even at his best, man has but a fading glory. He is likened in Scripture to the flower of the grass, bright but brief, transparent as a blossom maybe, but also as transient, a moment fair but soon to fade. In contrast, the eternal glory of Christ is ineffable in the effulgence of its perfect excellence; it matters not from which angle we approach the subject. We may contemplate the virtuous glory of His visage which is as voluminous as the corona of the sun, or consider the veritable glory of His vocation as Son of man, Servant, Shepherd, Saviour and Son of God. If we concentrate our minds on the vigorous glory of His voice which once shook the heavens, that created all and upholds all, for by that same word the world is kept in store until the consummation of the age, in this also Christ excels. Should we concern our attention with the vital glory of His victory, the wisdom of the Cross, the wealth of spiritual blessing secured and bestowed, and the wonderful gifts bequeathed as a result, Solomon is dimmed into utter insignificance. When we truly visualize how valueless we are individually, we get our first real vision of His true value, and of how virtuous and victorious He really is.

He is so infinitely gracious, inestimably precious and immortally glorious that we need to be strengthened with might by His Spirit in the inner man to be able to comprehend Him even in part. The floating iceberg has a far greater portion of its bulk submerged than that which is discernible above the water line. By far the greater degree of Christ's glory is still shrouded in mystery. The fraction that has been brought into manifestation is but a faint glimmer. So then the little that has been disclosed demands and deserves our fullest powers of observation, perception and comprehension, or we shall miss this many-splendored sight.

When the Prophet Daniel, the premier of Babylon, was given a glimpse of Christ's glory, he said his comeliness was turned into corruption (Dan. 10:8). This was not imagination but the illumination of illustrious glory. The disciples on the Mount of Transfiguration were startled as they gazed upon His raiment white and glistening. But what of the radiance of His intrinsic righteousness, the resemblance of His identical Godlikeness and the resplendence of His infinite greatness, in redemption, regeneration and reconciliation? Solomon had no power to comfort the brokenhearted in their sorrow, to cancel the sin of the guilty in their dilemma, or to conquer the gaunt enemy, death. Herein the glory of Christ transcends and exceeds the stars in excellence, and it never terminates, for there is nothing temporal and transient in His celestial character.

We need reminding that the essential nature of spiritual glory is for loving hearts to admire with reverent affection. The eternal Name of supernal glory with His continual revelations of richness is for the righteous to revel in. The everlasting fame of His sacrificial glory will ever be commemorated with adoration by myriads of the redeemed in His kingdom. We may say confidently without fear of contradiction that most graciously, most generously and most gloriously, Christ *is* greater than Solomon.

THE GREATER THAN JONAH

> The men of Nineveh shall rise up in judgment with this generation, and shall condemn it: because they repented at the preaching of Jonas; and, behold, a greater than Jonas is here (Matt. 12:41).

When our gracious Lord avowed Himself to be greater than Jonah He announced a tremendous claim. This Old Testament prophet preached in the central metropolis of

Gentile world dominion, after having encountered one of the most sensational experiences of any man in history. At the time Christ was speaking, He was about to startle the world with a far greater sensation by rising from physical death and emerging from a sealed tomb that was guarded by sentinels of the powerful Roman army.

He had plainly indicated during His ministry that after having been put to death He would return and exercise supreme power over both visible and invisible worlds. The great commission He gave to His disciples after His resurrection is a reverberating witness for all generations, in verification of the truth of His testimony (Matt. 28:18-20). Christ had in reality experienced death, burial and resurrection after which He ascended to the right hand of God. His disciples went forth, He also working with them, to engirdle the world with His message of redeeming love (Mark 16:19,20). Wherefore Christ is greater than Jonah in His superior personality.

No one ever made such prodigious and ponderous claims as Christ did. The statements He uttered were so profound that His words are not suited to the lips of any one else. Ordinarily it would be folly for greatness to exaggerate and fatal for honor to misrepresent anything. Any attempt to deceive mankind would lead to the frustration of the noblest design. But Christ's claim to power in heaven and on earth does not imperil authority but magnifies the majesty of its might a thousandfold. His claim to being the Son of God and Godlike is not detrimental to the faultless features of Deity but graces all heaven and glorifies Godhead. The claim He made, that He came not to be ministered unto but to minister and to give His life a ransom for many, does not misinform us as to God's character, but signifies that by substitutionary sacrifice God saves and secures the souls of men and sanctifies a host in order to found an eternal society. Our Lord's claim to riches in glory and the unlimited wealth of heaven does not disparage generosity but beautifies the beneficence of bountiful giving forevermore. His claim to receiving the commitment of all judgment as Son of man does no injury to justice but is the crowning justification of all divine adjudication.

Yea verily, the fourfold view of His superiority that is given in the final unveiling, where He is portrayed with the seven stars in His hand, the scroll in His hand, the sacred censer in His hand and the sickle in His hand, verifies forever that His claims are justified. These four famous figures of the Saviour portray Him as altogether worthy as Administrator of the Church, Executor of creation, Mediator in the commonwealth of nations and Adjudicator of the cities, both in the judgment of Babylon the great and justification of Jerusalem the glorious.

Christ is greater than Jonah in His sympathetic pity.

> So Jonah went out of the city, and sat on the east side of the city . . . till he might see what would become of the city (Jonah 4:5).
> And when He was come near, He beheld the city, and wept over it (Luke 19:41).

Jonah sulked because the city of Nineveh was not destroyed; Jesus sobbed because He saw the city of Jerusalem would be destroyed. "He wept over it": a world of wealth is contracted into these words. The whole strength of Christ's sympathy shone through the sorrow of His soul as He suffered the awful anguish of love's deepest agony. No metropolis ever saw such a Man: a mighty Monarch who had just participated in a triumphal march, immersed in tears; a merciful Mediator, grieving over the hardness and obduracy of a rebellious nation; a majestic Messenger, the King of meekness, brokenhearted over an impenitent generation.

The physical splendors of surrounding mountains and the material grandeur of the capital were altogether over-shadowed. The suitability of the site for the city of God, the sublimity of the spectacle in so comely a setting and the stately sanctuary as a citadel of worship had lost their charm. The moral conscience of Judah had gone; the spiritual tone of Jerusalem had perished. In the proportion in which these highest spiritual emphases of morality are no longer in the running of a city's administration, in that measure the nation has lost the grandeur of its greatness and the glory of its renown. Jerusalem had truly lost the loyalty of her love and her trust in the truth of God. The fear of God and flame of zeal no longer flourished in the temple courts. The trust of the true standards of weights and measures committed to temple custody for safeguarding right estimates of all dedicated things was no longer kept from abuse. The just balances of the sanctuary were soon to be used for the greatest injustice ever perpetrated. The high priest of the nation weighed thereon the thirty pieces of silver as a wage to a Simeonite to ratify a bargain for the promotion of treachery and betrayal.

Christ's unimpaired, unclouded, spiritual insight saw the future clearly. His undaunted interest in His people and His knowledge of the tragedy of tragedies about to occur might well cause Him to weep over the city. His infinite sympathy demonstrated itself in intensest grief; His was a grief we cannot grasp. No imposter could have endured such an ordeal. Even when treachery betrayed Him, obduracy defied Him, instability denied Him, timidity deserted Him, carnality despised Him, enmity derided Him and profanity mocked Him, His pity was unstaunched. "Behold, a greater than Jonas is here." Space forbids our considering Christ as being greater in submissive promptitude, steadfast purpose, serene patience, spiritual perception and sacrificial passion, in each aspect of which He far transcends the prophet who was sent to the Gentile world.

THE GREATER THAN JACOB

> The woman saith unto Him, Sir, Thou hast nothing to draw with, and the well is deep: from whence then hast Thou that living water? Art Thou greater than our father Jacob, which gave us the well, and drank thereof himself, and his children, and his cattle? (John 4:12)

The Bible contains numerous remarkable contrasts and comparisons in relation to Christ, each of which plays some part in setting Him forth to greater advantage. Maybe, had we been selecting characters from the Old Testament for the purpose of making such comparisons we would not have placed Jacob on the list. Unusual as it may at first appear, there is no other individual in the whole range of Bible history that contributes the fascinating features which are connected with Jacob's life, features which serve to bring into greater clearness the incomparable capability of Christ as the Regenerator and Reconciler of men.

After leaving home to seek a bride in Padan-aram, Jacob began his romantic career enroute, at a place he named Bethel, which means house of God. Here he experienced a startling surprise. On awakening he exclaimed, "Surely the Lord is in this place, and I knew it not." Jacob realized the fact of the omnipresence of God for the first time and also recognized the angel attendants. On the occasion of this supernatural vision, the Lord spake to him and said, "I am with thee, and will keep thee in all places whither thou goest . . . I will not leave thee" (Gen. 28:15). From this time forth he never lost the consciousness of God's presence. After marrying, he became the progenitor of twelve sons to whom he imparted his own human nature. Each son expressed one of Jacob's personal characteristics. The entire twelve in combination made up the full stature of their father.

Our Lord Jesus Christ, who came into this world to make known the reality of the omnipresence of God, commenced His public ministry, as recorded in John's Gospel, by drawing attention to the vision Jacob was given at Bethel (John 1:51). He then divinely demonstrated that presence at the marriage feast in Cana of Galilee, in the temple service and at the Passover commemoration. These three spheres express the society of the home, the sanctity of the Lord's house and security experienced in national history (John 2). Christ next introduced the teaching of regeneration in the new birth, and the significance of the brazen serpent uplifted (John 3).

In the following chapter He visited Samaria with His twelve disciples and after arriving at Jacob's well, which was near the parcel of land the illustrious patriarch had given to his favorite son Joseph, He was asked this question, "Art Thou greater than our father Jacob?" His reply was striking, for it indicated that Jacob's gift did not sustain Joseph but sufficed for his sepulcher. "My gift," said He in effect, "is a spring of life that will sustain and satisfy forevermore. Moreover I give with it the consciousness of the indwelling presence so that there will be no need to visit shrines and temples to worship the Father. They that worship Him must worship Him in spirit and in truth" (John 4:23-24). Indeed, He might have said, "Do you see these disciples that are with Me? I have made them partakers of My divine nature, so that it is possible for Me to say, Behold I and the children which God hath given Me" (Heb. 2:13).

How graciously and patiently Christ instructed Philip in Godlikeness, James in holiness, John in lovingkindness, Peter in graciousness, Matthew in meekness, Thomas in truthfulness, Nathaniel in guilelessness, Simeon in faithfulness, Jude in perfectness, Andrew in goodness, Thaddaeus in peaceableness and Paul in righteousness. These were twelve features of His own character and the twelve combined expressed His own person. This accounts for their names being engraved on the twelve foundation stones of the city of God. "Other foundation can no man lay than that is laid, which is Jesus Christ" (I Cor. 3:11).

In view of Christ having transformed these twelve men, a flood of light is thrown on His own divine character as the Regenerator. He made them what He is Himself, and the living stones bear witness that He is altogether precious as the perfect and permanent One, priceless in beauty and peerless in glory. The gorgeous colors of these twelve characters likened to jewels reflect the intrinsic values and inherent virtues of Christ's superexcellence; for He is the sum total of infinite spiritual perfection. As the component parts of Jacob's human nature were portrayed in his twelve sons, so the complement of the complete divine nature of Christ is fully displayed in His twelve sons. Behold, a greater than Jacob is here.

If such evidence fails to suffice, compare the testing of Jacob at Jabbok, and the testimony to Jesus at Jordan. Examine the character of the churlish enemy that departed from Jacob and the company of angels that reassured him, with the character of the adversary that departed from Jesus and the angels that ministered to Him (Gen. 31:55; 32:1; Mark 1:13). Meditate on Jacob's vision of the way to God and Christ's version of the way to the Father (Gen. 28:12,13; John 1:51;14:1,6). Consider Jacob's recognition of the divine presence and Christ's revelation of that presence (Gen. 28:16; John 14:9). There will then be no need to ask, "Art Thou greater than our father Jacob?" In His fullness of privilege, faithfulness in promise, freeness of prerogative, freshness of perception beside His fruitfulness in progenitorship, Christ is decidedly and definitely greater than Jacob.

THE GAZELLE

> There be three things which go well, yea, four are comely in going: a lion which is strongest among beasts, and turneth not away for any; a greyhound; an he goat also; and a king, against whom there is no rising up. If thou hast done foolishly in lifting up thyself, or if thou hast thought evil, lay thine hand upon thy mouth (Prov. 30:29-32).

The Hebrew word rendered "greyhound" is better translated "gazelle" — the fleetest-footed animal in the extensive deserts to the north, east and south of Palestine. Dogs were given no place in the symbolism and service of spiritual realities (Deut. 23:18). This figurative representation of the Saviour stands in conjunction with three other picturesque features of His many-sided character: a lion, a he-goat and a king. The lion is used as a symbol of strength, the gazelle suggests speed, the he-goat signifies sure-footedness and the king stands for supreme sovereignty.

Undoubtedly these symbols represent the chief factors in successful administration. However, our purpose is to take them in their supreme function and meaning as applied to the Governor Himself. Each of the figures used is beautifully descriptive of the functions Christ fills in the discharge of the divine duties, for the fulfilling of which He dedicated His life and labors. The fourfold portraiture attracts our attention to consider the mastery of His prevailing as the Lion, the ministry of His purpose as the Gazelle, the mystery of His passion as the He-goat and the majesty of His power as the King against whom there can be no rising in revolt.

We may say with confident certitude that the strongest, speediest, sturdiest and stateliest characteristics of strenuous service ever witnessed were expressed by Christ in His methods of ministry. The graceful comeliness and noble bearing of the Saviour's deportment are beautifully depicted, reflecting as these figures do, His charming supremacy, calm serenity, changeless security and consistent sovereignty. He soars loftily above all other leaders in high rank and real honor. Our Lord is always amiable in every activity He undertakes, He is forever admirable in every aspect of ability He exercises, He is universally available by virtue of the affinity He assumes as Son of man and He is most adorable because of the affable manner in which He ministers mercy from His throne of grace. How alert Christ is in His attentiveness toward the appeals of His people for help. How sincere His heart remains in the abiding affection of His love and how winsome is the attractiveness of His sterling goodness. Although He is supremely strong, He is nevertheless sympathetic, delicately sensitive but not touchy and sullen. He is steadfast in His wondrous purpose but not coldly cautious; He is resolute but not rough or resentful. He is sanctified in His consecrated devotion but not stiff and sanctimonious; He is fervent but not fickle. He is sovereign in His authoritative administration but not tyrannical; He is courageous but not contentious.

The richness of these simple figures reveals the celebrated One in the superiority of His strength as the lion which turns not away for any. He faces all our foes and gains a glorious triumph over sin, death, hell and the grave. Secondly, the covenanted One in all the sufficiency of His sympathy pursues the wayward, the wanderer and the willful. Yea, in this setting He is the stalwart seeker looking for the lost and making haste to forgive and receive all returning prodigals. He is as fleet of foot as the gazelle to overtake, bring back to the fold and transform the repentant. Thirdly, the consecrated One in the sanctity of His sacrificial love secures for man reconciliation and acceptance and acts for man in the matter of propitiation and substitution as reflected in the two goats of the great day of atonement, in the ceremonial of Israel (Lev. 16). Fourthly, He is the coronated One in the sublimity of His supreme rule, administering by virtue of His moral right and moral might in a kingdom free from riot and rebellion, immune from unrest and upheaval and devoid of all discontent and disruption.

What a store of wealth is resident in Christ to enrich, engrace and endow the people of God! In such instances as these we are introduced to the attributes of His kingliness, the attitudes of His kindliness, the attractiveness of His kinsmanship and the actualities of His kingdom. Surely if men knew the nature of His approach and the objective of His aim, all would readily yield to His claims.

THE GUIDE EVEN TO DEATH

> God is known in her palaces for a refuge . . . For this
> God is our God for ever and ever: He will be our guide
> even unto death (Ps. 48:3,14).

What an inestimable privilege it is to have a reliable Guide, in whom we may place the utmost confidence throughout the entire pilgrimage of life. Here we meet One who knows "The end from the beginning, and from ancient times the things not yet done, saying, My counsel shall stand, and I will do all My pleasure" (Isa. 46:10). He it is who undertook for Israel in their journey from Egypt to Canaan: He "made His own people to go forth like sheep, and guided them in the wilderness like a flock" (Ps. 78:52).

The particular word used for guide in Psalm 48 is variously rendered by such terms as "guided," "carried," "brought," "leadeth," "led," and so forth. A guide unto death is a figure indicating something entire and eternal. The Prophet Isaiah declares, "He that hath mercy on them shall lead them, even by springs of water shall He guide them" (Isa. 49:10). Both ideas of leading and guiding are found here and the figure is confirmed and completed in Revelation 7:17.

In order to grasp the precious character of this Guide, we should examine the whole Psalm 48. The opening verse introduces enthronement in the mountain of holiness; verses 3 and 8 carry us to enlightenment and establishment, which assure the enjoyment of verse 11. The encampment is emphasized by the use of "in" six times, and all this leads to endearment as in verses 9 and 14. "We have thought of Thy lovingkindness, O God, in the midst of Thy temple. According to Thy name, O God, so is Thy praise unto the ends of the earth: Thy right hand is full of righteousness" (vv. 9, 10). Therefore, "This God is our God for ever and ever; He will be our guide even unto death."

Surely His character of Guide should endear Him to all our hearts. What companionship! What communion! What compassion! Yea, and what compensation is entailed by having a Guide of such caliber as Christ the all-sufficient. He is an all-powerful, all-faithful, all-merciful, all-graceful, all-tactful, all-cheerful and almighty Guide. Why then should we be afraid to follow Him?

This wonderful Caretaker who guides, also guards us by His wise counsel; for the word "counsellor" is derived from the same root as "guide" and is so rendered in Psalm 32:8: "I will guide thee with Mine eye." He who has an all-seeing eye counsels us. Old John Wright said he had worked for his master so long that "all he wanted from him was a wink and he knew what to do." His wisdom is so sweetly loving, His words are so kindly true, His ways are so tenderly thoughtful and His will is so graciously perfect that we might well relish His company always.

In the book of Numbers, which records the history of His guidance of Israel through the wilderness, He continually went before to seek a resting place, but He also consistently acted as their rearward protection (Exod. 14:19-20). They likewise had with them constantly the symbols of His unfailing presence in the pillar of cloud by day and of fire by night; His unabating supplies of sustenance in the manna morning by morning; His untiring patience to meet their discontent; and His unceasing providence assuring water supply, weather conditions and watchful care suited to their needs.

We, too, are pledged guidance, "The meek will He guide in judgment; and the meek will He teach His way" (Ps. 25:9). We likewise are guaranteed the assurance of His presence, "I will never leave thee, nor forsake thee . . . The Lord is my helper, and I will not fear what man shall do unto me" (Heb. 13:5-6).

We cannot reiterate all His provisional guidance, for He led Israel to their forty-two encampments during the wilderness journey and recorded them as a demonstration of His unerring judgment (Num. 33). He registered the conditions when they commenced the journey and had an outline taken of the name, age and ability of each one. He recounted the circumstances by the way for teaching and testing them and recorded the characteristics that pertained at the consummation, at which stage they were compensated according to loyalty, activity and ability expressed by increase and numerical gain.

We likewise are to be rewarded according to what kind of work and how much of it we do. All results are dependent on the attitude held toward the steadfast Guide and stalwart Guardian who pledges to be our Leader and Counsellor to the terminus of this transient pilgrimage and will then receive us into everlasting habitations. We all may know His daily guidance via the channels of communion, conscience and circumstances. Gideon sought all three and secured them to make his venture sure of victory. The chief and choicest method of obtaining guidance is by the first of these three. When we commune with Him, He speaks to the conscience through His Word, and when we act, the circumstantial confirmation will not be lacking. Let us not begin with the latter for then we are simply as horse or mule that need the tug of the bridle to teach them which way to turn. Seeing we have such a gracious Guide, let us the more venerate His presence which is so real, value His promises which are so true, visualize His purpose which is so clear and voice His praises which constitute our supremest joy.

THE GOVERNOR AMONG NATIONS

> All the ends of the world shall remember and turn unto the LORD: and all the kindreds of the nations shall worship before Thee. For the kingdom is the LORD's: and He is the governor among the nations (Ps. 22:27, 28).

Government is a grand theme, but it is also the sphere where many of the fondest human hopes have been wrecked. The outstanding experiences of Old Testament history supply an outline of the everchanging nationalistic and socialistic systems of human administration which stand in sharp contrast to the unvarying sovereignty and unwavering stability of the government of God. Periods of righteous rule, of relapse and of reformation occupy the major portion of the records of Israel. The failure of many of the governors through incapability and insufficiency is abundantly offset by the portrayal of Messiah the faithful, whose character and capability assure us that He is perfectly qualified to govern. Christ can never be handicapped through indifference and indulgence, nor is He ever hampered by intellectual deficiency or moral delinquency.

Man's supreme need in all of his interrelationships is government; therefore this holds a special place in the purpose of the divine manifestation. The profoundest of the prophets of Israel proclaimed it: "The government shall be upon His shoulder . . . of the increase of His government and peace there shall be no end, upon the throne of David, and upon His kingdom, to order it, and to establish it with judgment and with justice from henceforth even for ever" (Isa. 9:6-7). The princeliest of the angelic host announced it: "He shall be great, and shall be called the Son of the Highest: and the Lord God shall give unto Him the throne of His father David: and He shall reign over the house of Jacob for ever; and of His kingdom there shall be no end" (Luke 1:32-33). The potent prayer of Messiah assures it: "Thy kingdom come. Thy will be done in earth, as it is in heaven . . . for Thine is the kingdom, and the power, and the glory, for ever" (Matt. 6:10,13). The paramount Apostle to the Gentiles affirmed it: "He hath appointed a day, in the which He will judge the world in righteousness by that man whom He hath ordained; whereof He hath given assurance unto all men, in that He hath raised Him from the dead" (Acts 17:31). The perfect apocalypse of Christ declares it: "And the seventh angel sounded; and there were great voices in heaven, saying, The kingdoms of this world are become the kingdoms of our Lord, and of His Christ; and He shall reign for ever and ever" (Rev. 11:15). "Thou hast taken to Thee Thy great power and hast reigned" (Rev. 11:17). The whole corroborative witness of the Scriptures points to a unified world-kingdom under the administration of Christ.

Man himself realizes this great need and has determined his own world project that one State must be supreme, all must subscribe to it, everyone must be subservient to it and every source of supply must be harnessed to sustain it. The ideal is all right but the incapability of man to establish it has been obvious from the time of Nimrod in Genesis 10 to the latest attempt in our own day. God's answer to such efforts is plain: "I will overturn, overturn, overturn it: and it shall be no more, until He come whose right it is: and I will give it Him" (Ezek. 21:27). The Apostle Paul clarifies the atmosphere for us to comprehend God's purpose more readily: "Having made known unto us the mystery of His will, according to His good pleasure which He hath purposed in Himself: that in the dispensation of the fulness of times He might gather together in one all things in Christ, both which are in heaven, and which are on earth, even in Him" (Eph. 1:9-10). The sovereignty of Christ's authority will then be manifest, the suzerainty of His farflung kingdom will prevail, the sufficiency of His governing resources will endure forever, while the superiority of His rule will subdue all other authority and power.

On account of our Lord's wielding supernatural powers, we are confident that of the increase of His government and peace there can be no end. When Christ governs, mankind will experience the centralization of all power, the consolidation of abiding peace, the confirmation of assured permanence, the certification of abounding perfectness and He will also be the criterion of age-long pleasure.

If we consider the values of the name of this Governor and the virtues of the nature of His government, we may fully account for the durable character of His dominion (Isa. 9:6). The very title, Everlasting Father, denotes that His authority is paternal, eternal and supernal. Herein we find harmonized gentleness as well as greatness, kindliness as well as kingliness, loveliness as well as lordliness, preciousness as well as powerfulness, friendliness as well as fatherliness and attractiveness as well as almightiness, humaneness as well as holiness, so that the factors that make for peace and guarantee its increase are resident in the Governor Himself.

In view of these inherent capacities He can never be defeated in purpose, never be dethroned by power, never be deflected by perversity and never be defiled by pollution. He abides unfalteringly in His stature of virtue, He administers unfaintingly in His state of virility and He stands unfailingly in the strength of victory.

> Look, ye saints, the sight is glorious,
>   See the "Man of sorrows" now;
> From the fight returned victorious.
>   Ev'ry knee to Him shall bow.

In the Psalm from whence we derive the title Governor among Nations, Christ bears the brunt of the cruelest violence and is made the butt of the direst injustice. Therefore He is a worthy candidate for governorship, for He realizes full well the envy and enmity of the enemy He intends to subdue. The supreme Sufferer becomes the serene Sovereign, the earnest Seeker becomes the excellent Singer and the stricken Saviour becomes the strong Subjugator. We may trace similar features in the New Testament. His crucifixion at the hand of man leads to His coronation at the right hand of God. His vicarious sacrifice for the guilt of mankind leads to His administration in the glory of majesty. His sufferings in bearing the penalty for sin lead to His sovereignty in the power of Saviourhood. No one had previously appeared on earth who foreknew the purpose of God, who foresaw the prevailing of grace and truth and who foretold the glorious triumph of an everlasting kingdom. The prerogatives of Christ entitle Him to supreme authority as Governor among Nations.

The Apostle John graphically describes Him in the tenth chapter of the book of Revelation, just prior to His taking to Himself His great power to reign. John depicts Christ in angelic form, arrayed in a cloud with an adorning rainbow, the sign of the covenant about His head, His amazing face as bright as sunlight and His advancing feet like pillars of fire. Such an array of symbols of irresistible might and independent majesty was never before used anywhere to describe any other potentate. The completeness of His control is colossal and under His governorship righteousness reigns, peace prevails, truth triumphs, while grace is glorified in the display of eternal goodness.

Christ is gathering up all things under a single and unified control. In the process He is shaking all things that can be shaken, so that the things which cannot be shaken may remain. His perfect virtue is the source of His prevailing strength, His prescient vision is the secret of His permanent security and His persistent valiancy is the spring of His permanent stability.

THE GATHERER OF LAMBS

> He shall feed His flock like a shepherd: He shall gather the lambs with His arms, and carry them in His bosom, and shall gently lead those that are with young (Isa. 40:11).

Many great contrasts are given in the Scriptures but none is more attractive in its kindliness and charm than the one in this chapter, which depicts the Creator and Counsellor as the Shepherd and Comforter (Isa. 40:1,11,14,26). None other than the Creator of the tremendous luminaries in the heavens is He who gathers the tender lambs to His heart. He that calls the innumerable host of stars by name without omitting one calls His own sheep by name and leadeth them out (Isa.

40:26; John 10:3). "Let us kneel before the Lord our Maker. For He is our God; and we are people of His pasture, and the sheep of His hand" (Ps. 95:6-7). "Neither shall any man pluck them out of My hand. My Father, which gave them Me, is greater than all; and no man is able to pluck them out of My Father's hand. I and My Father are one" (John 10:28-30).

This is something blessed above all blessedness, and precious beyond all preciousness, more preferable to the soul than priceless pearls. If you believe the Lord's teaching that not a sparrow falls without the knowledge and notice of your Father which is in heaven, is He not far more interested in children? Verily; for He also said, "Take heed that ye despise not one of these little ones; for I say to you, That in heaven their angels do always behold the face of My Father which is in heaven" (Matt. 18:10). "Even so it is not the will of your Father which is in heaven, that one of these little ones should perish" (Matt. 18:14).

Mark describes how He took up the little infants in His arms and blessed them (Mark 10:16). The very deportment of the good Shepherd is so warm and winsome that little children are attracted, and He appeals to His disciples to induce them to come to Him. His great Shepherd heart is full of friendly love and kindly interest which young ones are quick to discern and He often suited His choicest sayings to the minds of tiny folk. Seldom do we find words of more than one syllable: "The Son of man is come to save that which was lost" (Matt. 18:11). "I am the door: by Me if any one enter in, He shall be saved, and shall go in and out, and find pasture" (John 10:9). "Then said Jesus unto them again, Verily, verily, I say unto you, I am the door of the sheep" (John 10:7).

How we should admire this infinite One whose love is so full of passionate desire for the young. Let us remember Christ is a Shepherd-King and He purposes to found an everlasting kingdom. Who, may we ask, has ever heard of a kingdom without children? Yea in His kingdom they will predominate.

In the present world the choicest charms characterize child life. Children are so full of play and cheerful mirth that to be among them is to be in the nearest spot to heaven we can find.

Young love is warmer, young memory keener, young eyes brighter, young hearts gladder, young life sweeter and young minds purer than those found in people of maturer years; wherefore to trifle with a child entails terrible condemnation. Christ taught that those that were guilty of such behavior would have been better off had they been drowned in the depths with a millstone about their neck (Matt. 18:6). It is a crime to cause a child to stay in the paths of wickedness.

What a sight it is to see the lambs cluster about the Shepherd. How readily the sheep follow suit. So Christ uses the occasion to impress upon mankind the claim of His right, the care of His might and the caress of His delight for all little ones (Matt. 19:13-15; Mark 10:13-16; Luke 18:15-17). The descriptions given in this connection furnish one of the prettiest scenes in the entire ministry of Emmanuel, and we can be sure from His note of certainty expressed in the word "verily," that He still blesses children (Matt. 18:3).

The great lesson He taught as He placed a little child in the midst finally decides the utter exclusion from heaven of all those who lack childlike susceptibilities. "Except ye be converted, and become as little children, ye shall not enter into the kingdom of heaven" (Matt. 18:3). A little child is teachable and is willing to listen to instruction; so must we! A little child is trustful and believes what it is taught, sincerely and genuinely; so must we! A little child is transparent, free of duplicity, double-dealing and feigning; so must we be, if we desire to enter the kingdom of heaven. All too often in maturer years hardness prevents a teachable attitude of mind, and haughtiness prevents trust. Furthermore hypocrisy too frequently displaces transparency and attempts are made to excuse and cover up faults. Wherefore, instead of being teachable, trustful and transparent we become hard, haughty and hypocritical. It becomes quite obvious that if we are to enter the kingdom, we need to be made over again, which Christ terms "being born again."

The heart of the great Shepherd is particularly set upon children; therefore when His disciples attempted to send them away as intruders, they experienced one of the sharpest rebukes of His indignation. Had it been a delegation of judges seeking an interview, all would have been well; but a group of juveniles was of small account. His disciples thought Him too dignified to bother with little ones, while they considered lawyers and officials suitable for an introduction. In other words, the chiefs of congress were free to approach, but not the children of common folk. How valiantly and deliberately Christ upheld the children's right of access, and just think of the wide divergence there is between His dignity and that of the disciples.

When children are taught about the love that sought them and the work Christ wrought to save them, they are more deeply impressed than adults. When they hear the precious message about His blood that bought them and His grace that brought them nigh, they are deeply moved. God made us all sensitive to divine things. His weather signals are still real to the salmon and seals on our coasts. The humming birds and swallows know their appointed seasons, but men become hard and indifferent, and do not consider (Isa.1:3; Jer.8:7). Children are most impressionable, for the clay is as yet pliable.

The day will one day break and the morn will dawn when the Chief Shepherd will appear and end the rampage of the enemy. In the meantime this great Shepherd in His solicitous care for the lambs heeds their cries and helps those that suffer hurt. His gracious ministry of seeking, drawing, saving, sustaining and gathering goes on without let or hindrance. In His final commission to Peter, before He ascended, Jesus said, "Feed My lambs" (John 21:15). His own riches and resources for supply are replete. He provides rest and refuge amid the calm tranquillity and contentment of home. He readily ministers all requisites and spares no effort to satisfy His little ones. He is fully capable of fulfilling all obligations He undertakes, including the peace He pledges, the purpose He proposes, the power He proffers, the presence He promises and the place He prepares for an eternal habitation. He is strong to safeguard from the snare and storm, and His penetrating discernment enables Him to deliver from danger. David the shepherd of Israel had the skill to rescue from the jaws of the lion and paws of the bear, but Christ ransoms from the hand of Hades and redeems from death (Hos. 13:14). He is well able to meet all need and to feed and lead the lambs of His flock. At the final consummation of the age the most conspicuous multitude in the kingdom of heaven numerically will be made up of children; namely, the lambs which this Chief Shepherd has gathered home.

THE GLORIOUS LORD

> Who is like unto Thee, O LORD, among the gods? who is like Thee, glorious in holiness, fearful in praises, doing wonders? (Exod. 15:11)

> But there the glorious LORD will be unto us a place of broad rivers and streams (Isa. 33:21).

The word "glorious" is used twenty-one times in the Old Testament and most of the references refer to either the character or characteristics of the Lord. He Himself is the glorious Lord (Isa. 33:21), with a glorious name (I Chron. 29:13) and in His character He is "more glorious and excellent than the mountains" (Ps. 76:4). The superlative beauty of His divine characteristics include His glorious honor and majesty (Ps. 145:5,12), His glorious apparel and arm (Isa. 63:1,12), also His glorious kingdom, power, holiness, rest and sanctuary. If we are exercised in the contemplation of our Saviour's glory, we are already on the highway that leads to what the Apostle Paul describes as, "the excellency of the knowledge of Christ Jesus my Lord" (Phil. 3:8).

The first setting of the title, The Glorious Lord, is connected with the mighty deliverance Jehovah wrought from dominion of Pharaoh in Egypt. At a time when Israel was fettered by tyranny and chained in slavery, under bondage to the greatest world power of the early centuries, Jehovah pledged a visitation, and what He purposes is wholly reliable. His promises are the essence of truthfulness, the soul of faithfulness and the heart of trustworthiness. He first moved His people to a vantage ground where it was impossible for anyone but Himself to vindicate His faithfulness and verify the veracity of His promise. When the hour arrived He hastened to honor His word and directly and deliberately intervened to defend His people against the oppressor. The loftiest expectations of the people were exceeded and their highest hopes excelled.

In view of the great deliverance God wrought, Moses wrote his immortal song of commemoration which begins, "I will sing unto the Lord, for He hath triumphed gloriously." Moses magnifies the majesty of the Most High not so much for the display of mercy as for the demonstration of His might, the might of infinite power, which effectually interposed between the foe and the fugitives. What Moses witnessed fused the whole of his being into a praiseful frame and fanned his soul into a patriotic flame, intense with poetic fervor. He visualized the greatness of God, who had marshalled the celestial squadrons of His mighty ones to battle, even those loyal battalions who wield invisible powers, and this He did in order to demonstrate His great salvation. All of Egypt's captains, cohorts and chariots alike succumbed in the overthrow. The four "I wills" of the enemy's defiance and disdain were soon disposed of by the Almighty (Exod. 15:9). Moses was absolutely assured that no foe could snatch the conquest from the victor's hand, nor wrench away the crown of triumph won; so he reaches the superlative note in His immortal song with a challenging ring, "Who is like unto Thee, O LORD, among the gods? who is like Thee, glorious in holiness?" (Holiness is that wholesome rectitude of character which inspires righteousness of conduct in completeness and perfectness at all times and under all circumstances.)

On six other significant occasions during the history of the nation this same expression, "Who is like unto Thee?" occurs. In each instance the incomparable Lord is credited with activities that no one but Himself could undertake. In this case, the magnificence of the might that wrought deliverance becomes the subject of majestic music that never dies away. A multitude of multiplied millions beside the crystal sea of regenerative commemoration is revealed as participating in singing the song of Moses and the song of the Lamb, while they celebrate the two greatest deliverances, both national and universal that were ever wrought for mankind (Rev. 15:2, 3). The lesser triumph of Exodus at the crossing of the Red Sea foreshadowed the greater victory of emancipation achieved by Christ at the Cross for all mankind, a victory over the infernal powers of evil. This also had its memorial throughout all generations. The partial leads us to the perfect, the foreshadow directs to the full substance and the temporal finds its finality in the eternal.

How expressively and exclusively Moses attributes all honor to the glorious majesty of the Lord. This method of ascription is the more pronounced in the record of the great unveiling of our righteous Lord's triumph in His final victory over lawlessness. John witnesses to Christ in a threefold manner. He presents Him glorious in character, glorious in conquest and glorious in coronation with many crowns. Spontaneously the hosts of heaven give Him all the glory because He overcame the world, overthrew Babylon the great, overpowered the Wicked One and overpaid the enormous debt of sin by the riches of His moral wealth. His pristine glory becomes manifest in amaranthine splendor. As fairest of the mighty and strongest of the brave, His many conquests have made Him great in the eyes of all the redeemed. His victories have gained Him fame throughout the whole heavenly realm and His triumphs have won for Him celestial and terrestrial renown forevermore. Myriads now comprehend Him as the Altogether Lovely One who holds the almighty scepter and sways absolute sovereignty in age-abiding administration. His many diadems are studded with the diamonds of deity, the jewels of justice, the pearls of paradise and the gems of glory. The titles of royalty rightly belong to our Redeemer because of His regal righteousness which authorizes Him to reign as King of kings and Lord of lords (Rev. 19:16).

The essential excellence of His eternal majesty towers loftily above all other principalities and powers. Everything about His comeliness is durable and dignified. He it is who made the starry worlds and by His might upholds them. His wisdom weighs and balances the clouds. He hemmed in the seas with bounds and demonstrated when on earth that He can hush the billows to rest. In the hollow of His hands He holds the winds.

So we find grouped among His many distinctions the crown of creation, the miter of mediation, the robe of redemption, the scepter of salvation, the garland of grace, the coronet of conquest, the trophy of triumph and the diadem of dominion. Right worthily He bears this insignia, The Glorious Lord. Here it is we meet with One who dwells in the self-existent radiance of light eternal, who delights in the self-subsistent reality of life everlasting and who displays the self-sufficient royalty of love evermore.

We have been permitted the privilege and pleasure in these pages of presenting partially some of the peerless perfections of our all-glorious Lord and Saviour. The more we learn of Him, the easier it becomes to resign the temporalities of time and to commit the soul wholly to Him, whose pre-eminent power, permanent grace and prevalent truth abide the ages. All that is fairest, finest and firmest resides in the infinite, ineffable Christ. None can equal Him in excellence; for He is exempted from all comparison (Isa. 40:18). He exceeds all others in magnificence; for in essence He is the essential life, light and love of the Eternal (Heb. 1:3). In His own replete refinement as the Refiner of men, He removes all dross and defect; so that we may enjoy perfect participation in holiness. What a prospect is this! We are destined to embrace entirely His divine nature, be endowed with His perfections and enriched with His beauty. In such features there can be no dissolution or disruption and certainly no decay.

Let us therefore stand undismayed and undisturbed; for Christ the pre-eminent One prevails forever and ever.

Wherefore:

UNTIL WE KNOW that His omnipotence is overthrown, let us worship Him.

UNTIL WE HEAR that His almightiness is abolished let us revere Him.

UNTIL WE SEE that His immutability is imperiled let us believe Him.

UNTIL WE FIND that His unchangeableness is undermined let us trust Him.

UNTIL WE READ that His covenant is cancelled let us bless Him.

UNTIL WE LEARN that His superiority is superseded let us extol Him.

UNTIL WE SENSE that His faithfulness is failing let us follow Him.

UNTIL WE DISCERN that His dominion is declining let us serve Him.

UNTIL WE FEEL that His kingdom is crumbling let us obey Him.

UNTIL WE PROVE that His everlastingness is effervescent let us consult Him.

UNTIL WE DEEM that His purpose is paralyzed let us praise Him.

UNTIL WE DETECT that His throne is usurped let us glorify Him.

UNTIL HIS PLEDGE is fulfilled in the kingdom of God let us honor Him.

If it were possible for us to weigh the worth of Christ's worthiness, measure the magnitude of His meekness, recount the resources of His righteousness, perceive the perfection of His preciousness, trace the treasures of His truthfulness, grasp the glories of His goodness, ascertain the authority of His almightiness and determine the depths of His devotedness, the ultimate calculation would defy all human expression. All His attributes are timeless, changeless and ageless in their character.

"But the God of all grace, who hath called us unto His eternal glory by Christ Jesus, after that ye have suffered a while, make you perfect, stablish, strengthen, settle you. To Him be glory and dominion for ever and ever. Amen" (I Pet. 5:10, 11).